Barbara Randle's
more CRAZY QUILTING

©2005 by Barbara Randle
Published by

kp books
An Imprint of F+W Publications

700 East State Street • Iola, WI 54990-0001
715-445-2214 • 888-457-2873

Our toll-free number to place an order or obtain a free
catalog is (800) 258-0929.

Library of Congress Catalog Number: 2004097732

ISBN: 0-87349-975-1

Edited by Susan Sliwicki
Designed by Kara Grundman
Printed in China

Dedication

This book is dedicated to:

- My many sewing friends who have fallen in love with this wonderful old art called crazy quilting;
- My wonderful friend, Nancy Zieman, who has guided me almost from the beginning of my journey;
- My husband, Ed Randle, who always encourages me to continue; and
- Mrs. Violet Hopping, who has inspired me all of my life, and who continues to do so.

Acknowledgments

I am grateful to the many people who came together with me to make this book happen. Thanks to my friends, Pat Numnum, Yukie McLean, Sandra Morgan and Patty Vann, who have counseled and encouraged me through the process of preparing this book; my friends and relatives, Becky Jones, Linda Sims, Boo Bailey, Linda Medley, Teresa Real, Morgan Freeman, Kelly Vandiver and Linda Burns, who allowed us to photograph crazy quilt art in their homes; and my friends, Gale Roth, Pat George, Rhonda Hughes, Laura Thompson, Stacy Soeten, Pete Partin, Betty Bussey, Sharon Graham and Clark Underbakke and his 2003 second-grade class, for the contribution of their work and time.

Thanks to my friends at KP Books: Julie Stephani, who has offered valuable advice; my editor, Susan Sliwicki, who always was there when I called; and Bill Hahn, publicity, for all of his help.

Thanks to the many students who attend my classes and continue to inspire me. Thanks to my family for their patience and input. Last but not least, I wish to thank Sylvia Martin. Not only is she a fabulous photographer, she's a friend and so much fun to be with.

Table of Contents

Introduction

Colorful threads, projects and fabrics fill the ample workspace at the B. Randle Designs studio.

For years, after going from one creative outlet (could be called disaster) to another, I finally discovered crazy quilting. It was love at first sight — it felt like a favorite pair of house slippers after a long day of standing on concrete! It fits just right and finally fills that hole in my creative soul.

I've never been able to fully express it, because I couldn't identify what it was, but from very early in my life there were so many questions. Growing up, I remember the wonderful food that my mother prepared. She made the most delicious meals, and there was always a homemade cake. But the cakes were always pound cakes. (No complaints, you understand, just questions.) The wonderful aroma of pound cake cooking in the oven always brings back memories of home.

I never said it, but I always wondered why you would make a cake and not put icing on it.

And why would someone ever paint a room gray or tan when they could paint it yellow or turquoise?

And why wouldn't you always wear makeup with blush, eye shadow and mascara? And if eye shadow has glitter in it, why wouldn't you rather wear that?

Even the way people dressed — I always wondered why you would wear black or white when you could wear pink.

And if you were going to have a new pair or shoes, why would you choose black when the same shoe came in pink, orange or green — or all three?

And why doesn't everybody drive a convertible?

And if you could listen to music, why would there ever be silence? And if you could tap dance, why wouldn't you?

And why would you wear plain jewelry when you could wear sparkly rhinestones?

We'll never know why people do what they do, but, for me, I choose to embellish.

Since I "found" it only five years ago, my life has changed. And when I say changed, I mean really changed. I had accepted that sewing was a humdrum activity that I did for one of two reasons. I sewed to accomplish something that was one of life's necessities, like hemming pants, sewing on buttons or mending; or I sewed to save money, i.e., drapes, dust ruffles, slipcovers, pillow shams, etc. I had not experienced the world of "art sewing." Sewing was not something I did to fulfill a creative need. I did not know who Nancy Zieman or Martha Pullen were. I never had seen Threads magazine. I never had heard of couching, sew and flip, reverse bobbin work or the concept of sewing on a foundation fabric. My sewing world consisted of making piping, cutting out circular

tablecloths, covering cushions, making throw pillows and (ugh) hemming pants! Oh, and since I knew how to sew, people were always asking me to do little things, like "Take these pants in a little bit," or "Just shorten this knit shirt an inch." Is there any wonder I was bored with sewing?

There is one thing that has not changed in my creative world in connection with what I'm doing now. I always have loved fabric. I love to look at fabric. I love to touch fabric. I daydream about fabric. There is nothing like it. It's all about the possibilities. If you're like me — an artist at heart — fabric is your medium, the sewing machine is your paintbrush, and the sky's the limit!

I have gone from being a morning person to being a morning and night person. I used to go to bed early and get up early. Now I go to bed late and get up early! I am dreaming constantly about what's next: color combinations, new designs, and new ideas for projects, trims, tassels, decorative threads, yarns and software. The dam has broken!

Writing my first book, "Barbara Randle's Crazy Quilting With Attitude," was a scary experience for me, because I really didn't think I could do it. It wasn't until I actually saw the printed book that I believed! Now, with a little more confidence and the passion that I feel for my art, I am sharing more of the same.

Nothing has changed with regard to the basics. I again will share with you the how-to of crazy quilting and embellishment. But I also will walk you through the basics of making bags, explain how to create your own purse patterns, introduce brand-new purse designs and share a gallery of crazy quilted home decor items, garments and other cute stuff. You will find that this book is more personal than my first; you will see more from the heart.

I again have enlisted the services of Sylvia Martin to photograph my work. I think you will agree she is the best. The photography is done on location at some of the homes of my Crazy Quilt Friends, as well as my own home. It is my hope that you won't just look at the photographs. My goal is to have you read the words and be inspired to try the projects. I still believe that crazy quilting, with the possibilities of all the embellishments and wonderful fabrics, is the most fun that you can have with a sewing machine.

Getting Started

The concept of crazy quilting involves sewing pieces of different fabrics together and to a foundation to create a one-of-a-kind fabric. The method used to accomplish this is called Sew and Flip. In this chapter, you'll learn more about the basics of crazy quilting, ranging from techniques to tools.

FABRIC

Just looking at a crazy quilt, it seems that each piece of fabric is sewn together with another, then another, and on and on, until all fabrics, all going in different directions, are large enough to make this very large quilt. This would be the logical way to do it, based on the way traditional quilting is done.

However, knowing how fabric pulls when placed on the bias, it just doesn't make sense that these fabrics would "behave" if sewn like a traditional quilt. And so, it is no surprise that these randomly placed fabrics "act" better if sewn to a stable foundation.

FOUNDATION FABRIC

The weight of the foundation fabric is dependent upon the project. Stiffer or heavier fabrics provide more body; lighter fabrics are used when stiffness is not needed or wanted.

I use lightweight muslin for lampshades. The lighter the fabric, the more the light can shine through. For purses, I generally use heavy canvas. Muslin can be used, but depending on the weight of the fabric that is used for quilting, interfacing might be needed for body. I use organdy for some of my evening bags. Organdy is thin, but it has some stiffness. When in doubt, use lightweight muslin, and if more weight is desired, you can add interfacing as the item is being constructed.

The foundation always is cut at least 1" larger than the pattern. This is because some shrinkage usually occurs during the crazy quilting and embellishment processes. After all quilting and embellishment is done, press the work well. The finished fabric is treated like any purchased fabric. Place the pattern on the fabric, then cut. There is now a perfectly sized piece.

An example: For a 19" pillow top, which makes an 18" pillow, the foundation fabric must be cut 20" square. After crazy quilting, embellishing and pressing the 20" square, the pillow top is cut down to measure 19" square. This allows a ½" seam allowance all around.

QUILTING FABRIC

With crazy quilting, the rule for fabric is color. The more colorful it is, the better. Nothing gets the creative juices flowing faster than a wonderful piece of fabric.

I choose fabric mostly by the way it looks, not by the fiber content. If it has the luxurious look I want and it isn't too thick, I use it.

Designer fabrics made of cotton and polyester work well. Silks, taffetas, satins and brocades are always great. There also are many novelty fabrics on the market, including some that already have been embellished in some way. Tapestries are great if they are not too thick.

I have found that heavy fabrics just don't work well for me. And while I love velvet, it's not the easiest to sew. I don't use traditional cotton quilting fabric, except for lining some purses. I occasionally will use pieces of chintz or linen.

While fabric stores offer up plenty of choices, used and vintage clothing offer additional options for fabric. Shop in your closet for velvet, silk, brocade, taffeta and any other beautiful fabric from garments that might never be worn again but just keep hanging around.

TOOLS OF THE TRADE

Get every project off to a great start by gathering the basic tools and materials you'll need before you start to sew. These include:

- Sewing machine that can sew decorative stitches, has balanced tension and a sharp needle
- Pins
- Seam ripper
- Interfacing
- Fusible web
- Plastic canvas
- Thread
- Rotary cutter
- Cutting mat
- Scissors
- Ruler for use with rotary cutter
- Iron
- Ironing board
- Fabric marker
- Embellishments, including yarns, beads, tassels and trim
- Magnetic closures
- Purchased purse handles
- Webbing/ribbon

PROJECT GUIDELINES

Follow these basic guidelines for all of the projects in this book.

- Designs call for 44" wide fabrics, unless otherwise noted. Check the materials list for any notations about fabric width.
- Before you start a project, assemble the tools and supplies listed under Tools of the Trade. Be sure to check the materials list to find of which fabrics, notions, supplies or other items that you also may need.
- Take time to thoroughly press the crazy quilted fabric as you go. While it may feel like you're at the ironing board all of the time, good pressing will lead to great results.

CRAZY QUILTING TECHNIQUES

In this book, I refer to three different methods of crazy quilting: Traditional, Chevron and On the Slant.

As you will see, each method is different. However, one thing remains consistent in all three: Sew and Flip.

While piecing techniques are important, proper pressing plays a role in getting great results, too. To get a smooth finish, make sure the work is as flat as a pancake after you flip each piece and before you proceed with the next strip of fabric. Little tucks between fabrics can be unsightly and can make embellishment difficult. Remember, you are creating your own unique fabric design; the smoother the finish, the better.

METHOD 1: TRADITIONAL

The Traditional style of crazy quilting is the most common technique. This method is used for pieces that are symmetrical, and it is the one I use in all beginner classes. It starts with a centerpiece, to which fabric is added until the foundation fabric is covered. A four-sided centerpiece can be used, but more interesting angles can be achieved with a five-sided piece of fabric. Create a five-sided piece of fabric by cutting a square or rectangle the desired size, then clipping the fabric to make a fifth side.

1 Place the five-sided centerpiece onto the approximate center of the foundation fabric. To create more interesting angles on your finished work, angle the five-sided centerpiece so its edges don't line up with the foundation fabric.

2 Stitch the centerpiece to the foundation fabric. Sew along one of the centerpiece's long sides.

3 Cut a rectangle of another quilting fabric. Place the new rectangle, right sides together, on top of the first piece where it was stitched.

4 Sew the edge of the new quilting fabric rectangle to the foundation fabric, just above the original stitching, using at least a ⅜" seam allowance. Trim the edge to the seam allowance. Flip this piece over so the right side shows and the seam is concealed. Press the piece well as you go.

5 Cut and sew another quilting fabric rectangle using the Sew and Flip method, moving either clockwise or counter-clockwise. Press.

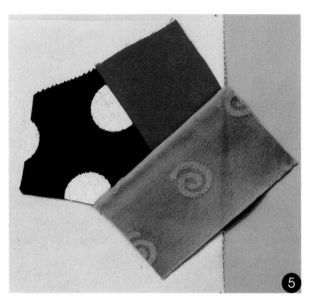

6 Repeat Steps 3, 4 and 5 to cover all raw edges until backing is totally covered. After each piece is sewn, trim the seam allowance. Do not trim too close to seam, as raveling might occur. Press.

Method 2: Chevron

Chevron-style crazy quilting usually is used on oblong or unusually shaped projects. I use this method on long and narrow rectangles, lampshades, scarves and other items that are not square. It can start at the center or at one corner of the foundation fabric.

1 Place a square in the center of the foundation fabric. On occasion, quilting may start on one end of the project instead of the center.

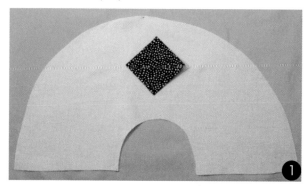

2 Use the Sew and Flip method and a ¼" seam allowance to sew fabrics around the centerpiece until the width of the foundation fabric is covered. Press the piece well as you go.

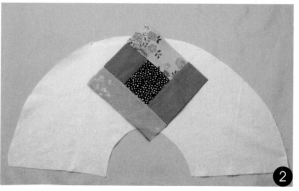

3 Continue adding quilting fabrics using the Sew and Flip method until one end of the foundation fabric is covered. Press.

4 Repeat Steps 1 through 3 for other end of the foundation fabric. Press.

Chevron-style crazy quilting often is used on oblong or unusually shaped projects, such as this lampshade.

METHOD 3: ON THE SLANT

While some may not consider it to be crazy quilting, the On the Slant technique is one I incorporate into my designs and use in many of my advanced classes. It is the simplest of all and goes really fast. I use the Sew and Flip technique when I am developing a new design. Long strips of fabric are placed on the diagonal. Because fewer fabric pieces are used, it takes less time to quilt. Strips can be all one width, or they can be cut different widths to add interest. Use this method on a foundation of any shape or size.

1   Place one strip diagonally in the center across the backing. Sew both sides of the strip to the backing, ⅛" from edges.

2   Place another strip on top of the first strip; keep right sides together. Sew from one end to the other, using a ¼" seam allowance. Flip and press.

3   Repeat Step 2, using the Sew and Flip technique to add strips until the backing fabric is covered. Press the piece well each time after adding a strip.

Embellishments: Decorate Your Life

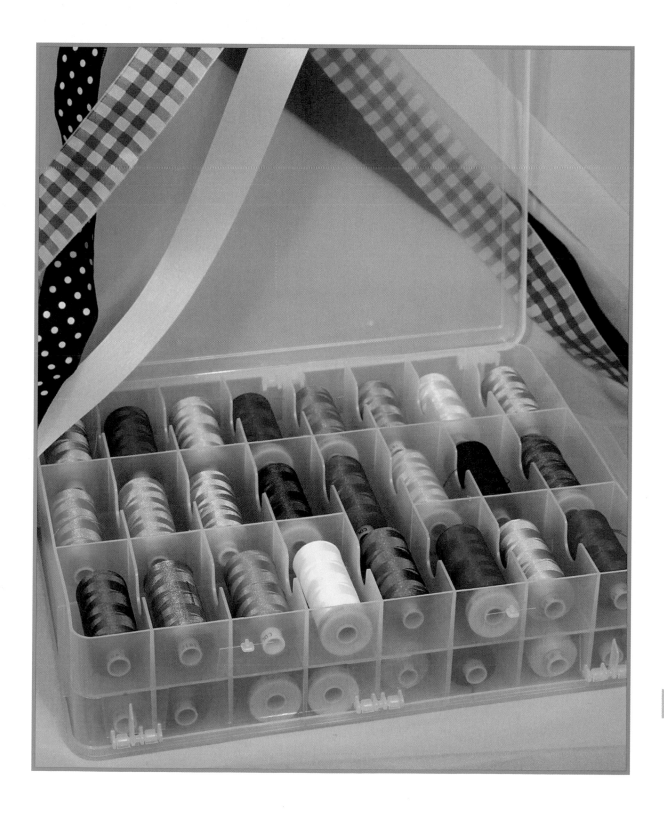

Enjoy an artistic feast when you crazy quilt; use fresh fabrics and fashionable fibers to add flavor to every project.

Embellishment is fun, whether you are decorating your life or a crazy quilted project. You might think that after five years I might have drifted away from crazy quilting, but I am still just as fascinated as I was when I first started. I think the fabrics, yarns and embellishments are "good enough to eat!"

Using so many beautiful yarns as embellishments might just inspire you to learn to knit. That has happened to me. It's great when you travel or at home when you're too tired to sew, but still want to do something. (I have learned to knit in bed!)

GET INSPIRED

As with everything in art, what we create is limited only by our imaginations. If you think your imagination is stuck and you'd like to get it unstuck, you can.

Just look around. Begin to change the way you look at things. Pay attention to details. Visit art galleries. Go to quilt shows. Study pictures in books and magazines.

These knitted scarves show some of the gorgeous yarns that also work well for embellishing crazy quilted items.

What are your true favorite colors? Are you afraid of color? If you love bright colors but never use them in your home or in your art, reach out and do something different. Loosen up. Take a chance.

You can change the way you use color in your life by developing color awareness. Embellishment is just decoration. When you buy a piece of artwork for your home, you are embellishing your home. When you look at a home-decorating magazine and you are drawn to a particular room or arrangement, look at everything in the photograph. Ask yourself what it is that caught your attention. Look at every detail; study the color of everything in the photograph. Then apply what you see in your own life.

Life is wonderful when lived in color. Here are some fun and easy ways to embellish your life:

Instead of hemming a too-long pair of pants, cut off the extra fabric and stitch a ruffle around the bottom.

Buy a round table, make a floor-length round tablecloth out of black and cream stripe fabric, and then crazy quilt a square to go on top, such as this one done by my daughter-in-law, Kelly Vandiver. Embellish it with heavy tassel fringe.

If you're a knitter, don't hide those beautiful yarns in a drawer. Roll colorful yarns into balls, put them in a large bowl or basket, and place them on a coffee table.

Dress up the dining room table with a crazy quilted throw, such as this one created by Teresa Real.

Randle's Rule

How to know when you've embellished enough: When it seems that there is enough embellishment on your work, add two more things!

GET READY TO EMBELLISH

The most popular class at B. Randle Designs Studio is the Square of the Month Class. Students come to class once a month for one year. They create a square at each class, and their homework each month is to embellish that one square. Some of these embellishments are hand work; some are machine work.

At the end of 12 months, students have created 12 squares that, when put together, create a 54" x 72" throw. These throws are incredible heirlooms, and each piece is as different as the person who created it.

In this chapter, I will share a little about hand and machine embellishments, as well as the instructions to create the throw, so you can try embellishing and crazy quilting for yourself.

PREPARE YOUR PROJECT

After I have finished crazy quilting, I steam and press the work to make it as flat as a pancake. Next, I serge or zigzag the outer edges to hold the fabrics in place as I embellish from the front or the back.

HAND EMBELLISHMENT

If you want instant gratification, you probably think hand embellishment is out. In reality, it can be done pretty quickly. Try hand embellishment, with or without an embroidery hoop. Start with embroidery floss and simple stitches. Then try ribbon embroidery.

The original, old-fashioned crazy quilts are completely hand embellished. It is amazing how perfect the hand stitches are on these old quilts. Search through books for pictures of antique crazy quilts, or visit art museums that have exhibits of antique crazy quilts.

Students enrolled in the Square of the Month Class receive "The Crazy Quilt Handbook, Revised, 2nd Edition" by Judith Baker Montano, a wonderful resource for detail on how to hand embellish crazy quilted items. Other good resources about embellishments are Quilting Arts Magazine and Deanna Hall West's book, "Encyclopedia of Ribbon Embroidery Borders."

Here are some samples of handwork completed on crazy quilted throws by students in Square of the Month Classes at B. Randle Designs Studio. Many students were new to handwork until they came to these classes.

Handwork by Morgan Freeman.

Handwork by Rhonda Hughes.

Handwork by Linda Medley.

Handwork by Laura Thompson.

Handwork by Linda Medley.

Handwork by Linda Medley.

MACHINE EMBELLISHMENT

As with the crazy quilting methods, these embellishment techniques are nothing new. These classic machine techniques illustrate how I create the "attitude" in my crazy quilting.

Many of the decorative stitches on today's dream sewing machines are modern replicas of the hand-quilted stitches found on antique crazy quilts. These same stitches can be sewn from the front of the work using regular machine embroidery thread in the top and a regular bobbin but with less impressive results.

Embellishment can totally change the way the work looks. When it comes to embellishment, I think more is better. Everyone who really gets into it will develop his or her own style. Some people like a lot of embellishment; some like a little. Crazy quilting with fabulous fabrics and no embellishment also can be very interesting.

Unembellished square by Barbara Randle.

Embellished square by Linda Medley.

REVERSE BOBBIN WORK

Reverse bobbin work is getting more attention. You can't beat it for getting a bold look very quickly. To do it, you must have a machine that has decorative stitches built in and is capable of doing reverse bobbin work. Heavy threads that can't go through the sewing machine needle or tension disks can be wound and used in the bobbin instead.

Many machines on the market today will do reverse bobbin work. If you are unsure whether your machine will, purchase a spool of thread and try it. Threads that I recommend using are Décor and Glamour by Madiera®, and Candlelight, Designer 6 and Pearl Crown by YLI®.

Two great machines that I have found for reverse bobbin work are the Artista 200 and 185 models from Bernina® and the Creative 2144 and 2056 models from Pfaff®. Both make the best and boldest stitches because they have 9 mm wide stitches. This is great for bobbin work, which is done on the back of the work, as well as stitches on the front of the work.

Some Baby Lock®, Elna®, Janome®, Brother® and Singer® models have 7 mm stitch widths, which is almost as good as the 9 mm width. The Bernina®, Pfaff® and Baby Lock® models also have a few large stitches that are up to 40 mm wide. Reverse bobbin work can be done using these stitches, and they look great.

Buy an extra bobbin case to be used only for bobbin work so you do not disrupt your regular sewing bobbin tension. Adjusting the tension on a bobbin case used for regular sewing can pose problems, because it is very difficult to get it readjusted for regular sewing, and eventually the threads could be stripped on the screw.

The way that reverse bobbin work is done depends upon the machine, but the basic steps remain the same.

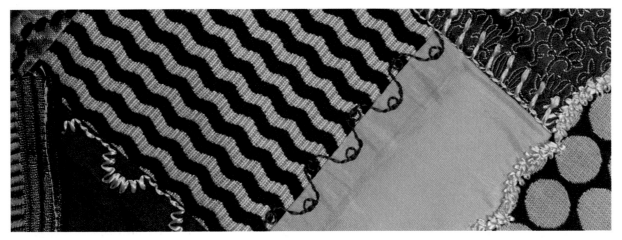

Reverse bobbin work.

TRY THE TECHNIQUE

1 Prepare the bobbin. If a machine with a drop-in bobbin is used, simply bypass the bobbin tension. If a machine with a bobbin case is used, purchase an extra bobbin case that is only used for bobbin work, and loosen the bobbin tension.

2 Wind the heavy, decorative thread onto the bobbin by hand. Use monofilament thread or matching all-purpose sewing thread through the top of the machine.

3 Select an open, decorative stitch from among those programmed in your machine. Avoid satin stitch designs or designs that have a lot of close stitches.

4 Flip the crazy quilted work over so the backside faces up. Stitch along the center of a seam line, following the seam lines on the back of the work. Each seam is a guide, or road map, of where to sew.

5 Once the decorative stitches are sewn, pull the ends of the threads through to the back of the work. Knot the threads to keep them from pulling back through to the front. Never back tack or lock the stitches when doing bobbin work.

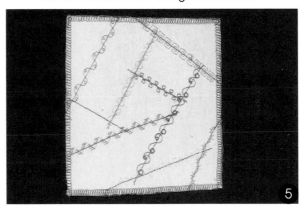

6 After stitching from one end of a seam to the other, turn the work over and enjoy the results. This bold stitch is actually the bobbin stitch. Try using a different decorative stitch on each seam.

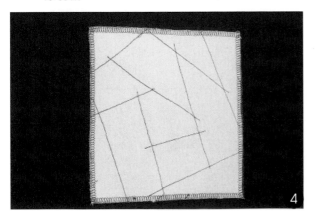

DECORATIVE STITCHES FROM THE FRONT

All machines with decorative stitches have satin stitches. If you are machine embellishing on the front of the quilt with 40-weight thread, the boldest stitches will be obtained by using satin stitches. Thicker 30-weight embroidery thread also is available; this thread works well for stitching on the top of the quilt. Thread for denim also works well for embellishing the quilt top.

The Pfaff® Creative 2144 has a series of stitches called antique quilting stitches. When sewn on the front of the quilt with 40-weight embroidery thread, these stitches are the closest I have seen to handwork.

DRIVING OR COUCHING

Driving yarn.

Driving.

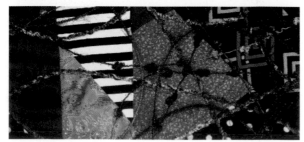

Heavy driving.

My definition of driving, or couching, is attaching yarn, decorative thread, found fiber or trim to fabric. You can do so by hand or machine, stitching at intervals along the yarn, thread, fiber or trim.

I use mostly yarns for driving. I love to use a yarn called Aura by Trendsetter®. I use it on almost everything; it has this little fiber that glistens. Sock yarn in a black-white combination is another real find. Local knitting shops are great sources for yarns. But be careful what yarns you choose. Heavy, thick yarns are unsuitable, and yarns with large bumps are difficult to sew onto fabric.

I have a love-hate relationship with monofilament thread. It can be very contrary, but it is a key element in successful driving. If there was no monofilament thread, we never could achieve the look of wonderful, colorful threads, yarns and fibers gliding over our work. The YLI® clear thread works best for me; it is softer and seems to work better in my machine.

Driving takes some practice. At first you might get jerky circles and lines. Just keep trying. I have found that the more I drive, the faster I can go, and the faster I can go, the smoother the lines. Remember to lengthen your stitch.

TRY THE TECHNIQUE

1 Put regular bobbin thread in the bobbin case and thread monofilament on the top of the machine.

2 Set your machine to a zigzag stitch. The stitch width depends on the material being couched onto the work. I find that lengthening the stitch seems to make the process smoother and quicker; it usually works well to use a stitch width of 3 mm and a stitch length of 3 mm. Increase or decrease stitch length or width as needed.

3 Starting at an edge, zigzag a piece of yarn onto the work. There is no plan — just circles, curlicues and whatever happens.

OTHER FUN EMBELLISHMENTS

There are so many more things that can be embellished onto crazy quilting. Just use your imagination, and most of all, have fun!

Here are some pieces for inspiration.

Pat George cut these butterflies out of a fabric with a butterfly print. They are hand stitched around the edges. Notice her beautiful embroidery work and the button embellishment.

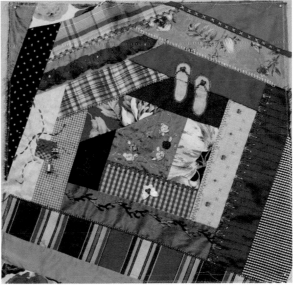

Gale Roth came up with the idea for the flip flops (top and above). They were appliquéd onto the square — so cute!

Linda Medley took apart silk flowers and hand stitched the petals to her quilt. A few beads were added for interest.

Laura Thompson put this fabric fan on the corner of a crazy quilt square.

EMBELLISHING SECOND-GRADE STYLE

When invited to speak to a class of second-graders about crazy quilting, I admit, I wondered how crazy quilting could be applied to a second-grade class. But, nothing is impossible where children are concerned. Little did I know that these second-graders, with very little help, would end up making a crazy quilt. The second-graders' journey into quilting began innocently enough, said teacher Clarke Underbakke.

"As a class, we were studying geometry. Frustrated and bored with the notion of creating a quilt out of construction paper, I summoned the help of parent Laura Thompson. Thompson, a student of Barbara Randle's, came with quilts and ideas in hand. Immediately, the class was hooked. Boys and girls alike were intrigued by the idea of creating a class quilt," Underbakke said.

Thompson helped each child create a crazy quilted square. After the squares were finished, she came to class every day for a week to assist in embellishing techniques that ranged from beads to sequins. The children added layer upon layer of adornment, and the squares began to take on the personalities of their creators. Once the squares were finished, they went home with Thompson's daughter, Hannah Kate, to be made into a quilt, Underbakke said.

"The atmosphere in the room the day of the completed quilt's arrival was nothing short of magical. As the quilt was unfolded, the children anxiously looked for their squares and admired the squares of their classmates. The project was a great success in all areas. Our study of quilts criss-crossed the curriculum. The connections to math being obvious, we also read all about quilts and their rich history — how quilts helped slaves escape to freedom via the Underground Railroad; how they were the lifeblood of the isolated community of Gee's Bend, Ala.; how each quilt offers a story, no matter how plain or fancy. Children brought in quilts and proudly told their own family histories. By authentic means the children had learned a great deal about geometry, color, pattern, following directions and the like. Most importantly, the children learned that like the quilts we studied, no matter how fancy or simple, we each play a vital piece in life," said Underbakke, who received the quilt as a gift from his students.

Second-grade student quilters who made blocks include (from left) Hannah Kate Thompson, Blake Norris, Ben Richey, Alex Watkins, Keanu Sida, Amelia Self, Reid Stewart and Caroline Conrad.

Buttons, beads and fabric paint were among the items Clarke Underbakke's students used to embellish their quilt.

Crazy Quilted Throw

Crazy Quilted Throw by Linda Sims. Finished size: 54" x 72".

Materials

Fabric

- 3½ yd. muslin (foundation)
- 2⅛ yd. backing fabric, 60" wide
- ⅓ yd. each of 26 different fabrics (crazy quilting)

Embellishments and Notions

- 3⅛ yd. bullion fringe or other trim (optional)
- Thread
- Other embellishments as desired
- 6 buttons

Making your own personalized throw is easier than you think. Here's a project to help you get up to speed on the basics of piecing and embellishing, crazy quilt style.

Embellishments are a highlight of Linda Sims' throw (above and top).

From	Cut
Muslin	12 squares, 20" x 20"
Quilting fabrics	12 squares, 5" x 5" (all from 1 fabric)
	100 selvage-to-selvage strips, 3" wide (4 strips each from 25 fabrics)

QUILT AND EMBELLISH

SQUARES

1 Crazy quilt one square. See Getting Started for details on crazy quilting methods.

2 Embellish the crazy quilted fabric as desired. See Embellishments for ideas and detailed instructions. Press well.

3 Trim the finished piece down to 19" square.

4 Repeat Steps 1 through 3 for the remaining 11 squares.

ASSEMBLE

THROW

1 Place two finished squares right sides together. Use a ½" seam allowance to stitch two squares together.

2 Sew another square to the unit to yield a three-square row.

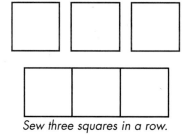

Sew three squares in a row.

3 Repeat Steps 1 and 2 to yield four rows of three squares each.

4 Sew the finished three-square rows together to create a 12-square throw.

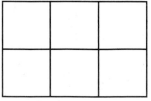

Join the three-square rows.

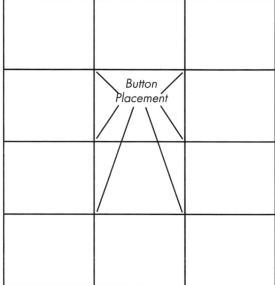

Top

Button Placement

Bottom

5 Lay the throw right side down onto the backing fabric.

6 Cut the backing fabric the same size as the throw.

7 If desired, stitch bullion fringe or trim onto the right side of the quilt. Place the trim 2½" from the top and bottom, with the band side placed toward the center of the throw.

8 With right sides together and with bullion fringe or trim turned up away from the seam, stitch the throw to the backing using a ½" seam allowance. Leave an opening on one side for turning.

9 Turn the throw right side out. Stitch the opening closed.

10 Use buttons to secure the throw front to the lining. Sew buttons at the intersections of the squares.

Throw by Boo Bailey.

Throw by Linda Sims.

Throw by Linda Burns.

29

Throw by Rhonda Hughes.

Throw by Boo Bailey.

Throw by Betty Bussey.

Bag Basics

Barbara Randle assists a student with a project at the B. Randle Designs studio.

You'll use several basic skills over and over again when you're making bags and purses. Refer to this section for specific tips on making handles, mitered purse bottoms, ruffles and pockets, and inserting magnetic snaps and purse bottoms.

Make your purse projects even easier by creating a kit for each one. Use each project's materials list as a checklist, then cut the fabrics and make the kit. This is much easier than stopping to cut as you go.

Linda Medley makes kits for classes at B. Randle Designs.

MAKING FABRIC HANDLES

Make your own handle from fabric and fusible fleece. Here are general instructions to create 1" wide fabric handle.

1 Cut one strip of fabric that is 4" wide by the desired finished length. Cut two strips of fusible fleece that are ⅞" wide by the desired finished length. Position the fusible fleece on each long edge of the wrong side of the fabric.

Fusible Batting
Center Fold Line
Fusible Batting

2 Fuse the fleece to each horizontal edge of the fabric strip.

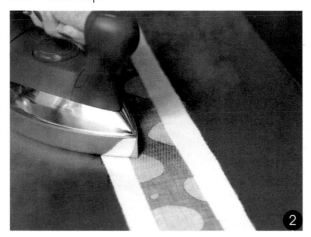

3 Fold the fabric in half horizontally. Press.

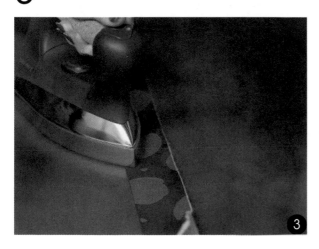

4 Fold the raw edges of fabric with the fleece toward the center. Press.

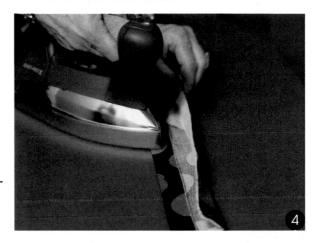

5 Fold the handle in half once more. Press.

6 Stitch the folded handle together along both long edges.

MAKING MITERS

A rectangular or square purse bottom can be made one of two ways. A separate rectangular or square piece can be set in, or a miter can be made that will form the rectangular or square bottom from the purse body. A miter is so much simpler to do; none of my designs have set-in bottoms anymore. Here are general instructions to create a 4" miter that will yield a purse bottom that is 4" wide.

1 Match the side seams of the pouch with the center of the purse bottom to form a triangle. If there is only one side seam and a crease on the other side, treat the crease as a side seam.

2 Pin the pieces in place to hold the position.

3 Make a mark 2" from the point of the triangle. Draw a 4" line across the triangle, which intersects the 2" mark; this line will be parallel with the point.

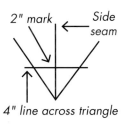

2" mark   Side seam

4" line across triangle

4 Stitch across the 4" line. If desired, trim the points of the miter.

USING GRID POCKETS

The "grid" is the material that I use to create a stiff bottom in my purses. I prefer plastic canvas, which is made for a type of needlepoint and can be purchased at craft stores. Plastic canvas is inexpensive and easily can be cut into any size with scissors. Other materials that can be used for purse bottoms include cardboard, foam core board and material used for plastic signs.

The idea for a grid pocket came from my friend, Kaaren Hopping. Originally, we just dropped the grid into the bottom of the purse between the lining and the purse. Very often it would creep up the side. Kaaren came to me after attending a class and suggested that a pocket to hold this piece would make sense. She was right, and now it is used in all of my purse designs that need a hard bottom.

To make a grid pocket, you will need the lining cut to size for the purse you are making, the piece of plastic canvas grid cut to size for the purse you are making, and another rectangle of fabric cut 1" wider and 1" longer than the plastic canvas grid.

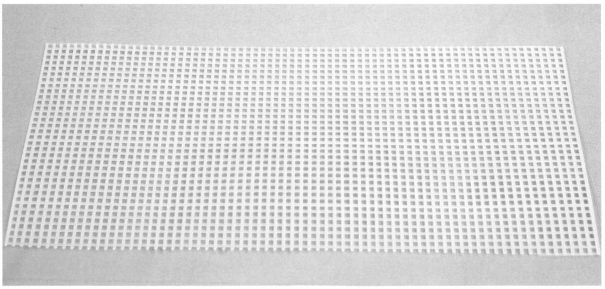

Plastic canvas adds strength and rigidity to purse bottoms.

MAKING GRID POCKETS FOR MITER-BOTTOMED PURSES

1 Make the lining by folding the lining fabric right sides together. Sew the ends to create a pouch.

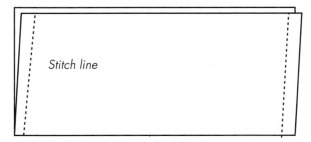

Stitch line

2 Sew miters at the bottom corners of the lining pouch to the size needed for the purse. See Making Miters for detailed instructions. Press a crease on each side to form the rectangular bottom.

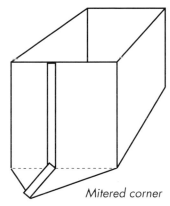

Mitered corner

3 Sew the base of the mitered lining pouch to the fabric rectangle, wrong sides together, along the long edges only to create a casing.

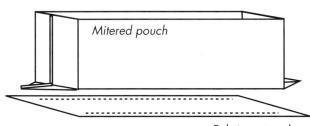

Mitered pouch

Fabric rectangle

Finished pouch and casing

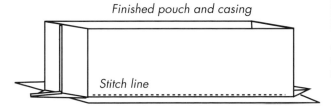

Stitch line

4 Lift the miters and insert the grid into the casing.

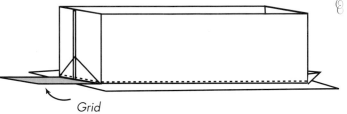

Grid

5 Tuck the miters inside of the grid-filled casing, beneath the grid. For extra strength, stitch the miter to secure the grid. Or clip the miters off, if desired.

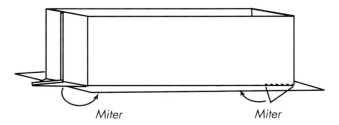

Miter   *Miter*

Plastic canvas adds rigidity and strength to the bottom of a handbag. A grid pocket sewn into the lining prevents the plastic canvas bottom from shifting out of place.

INSERTING MAGNETIC SNAPS

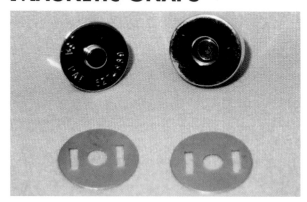

Magnetic snaps offer an easy option for purse closures.

There are four components to a magnetic snap: two parts with prongs that fit together that are actually seen inside the purse; and two holders, or parts that the prongs fit through, that go on the inside of the lining. These snaps generally are installed on the purse lining. Here are general instructions to install snaps.

1 Find the center front and back of the purse lining. Make a 2" vertical mark on the wrong side of the fabric. Make a horizontal mark on the front and back of the lining that is 1¼" down from the top edge.

Top edge

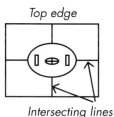

Intersecting lines

2 Center the female side of the magnetic snap over the intersection of the two lines. Use this as a template. Mark the lining.

2

3 Use two small pieces of interfacing on the inside of the lining to secure the holders over the intersection of the two lines. Use this as a template, and make pencil marks through the side slits onto the lining to mark the position.

4 Remove the holder. Use a seam ripper to carefully cut slits where the marks were made.

4

5 Put the prongs on the outer part of each snap through the slits from the outside of the lining. Use pieces of interfacing on the inside of the lining to help secure the snaps. Place the holder on the prongs on the inside of the lining. Bend the prongs so that they are flush with the holder; you can use a pliers to help you. Do not use a hammer, which could damage the snap.

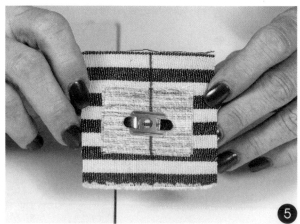
5

MAKING RUFFLES

1 Fold the ruffle fabric in half lengthwise, right sides together, matching long raw edges. Stitch the short ends together to finish them.

Fold the fabric, then stitch the ends.

2 Turn the piece right side out. Press the seams at the ends.

3 Serge or machine baste the raw edges to hold them together during ruffling.

4 Gather or ruffle the piece from the raw edges, manually or by machine, to create a ruffle.

Gather the ruffle.

MAKING POCKETS

1 Make a pocket by folding the pocket fabric in half vertically, right sides together.

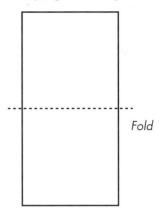

Fold

2 Stitch around three open edges, leaving small opening at the bottom to turn the pocket.

Leave open to turn.

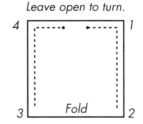

Fold

3 Turn the pocket. Press.

CREATE YOUR OWN DESIGNS AND PATTERNS

When I create a design, I usually am inspired by something. It might be my desire for a certain size, or it might be the need for an item with certain features. It even could be a shape. Whatever the motivation, it starts with an idea that progresses to paper, then to fabric. The results aren't always what I originally envision, as occurred when I was invited to teach a purse class at the Smocking Arts Guild of America's annual Sewing At The Beach event at Myrtle Beach, S.C., in January 2004. When I do a special event, I like to design a bag especially for the occasion and give it a name that reflects my mood or the venue. First I sketched the bag that would be called the Myrtle Beach Bag. Here's what my sketch looked like:

Myrtle Beach Bag, front view.

Myrtle Beach Bag, back view.

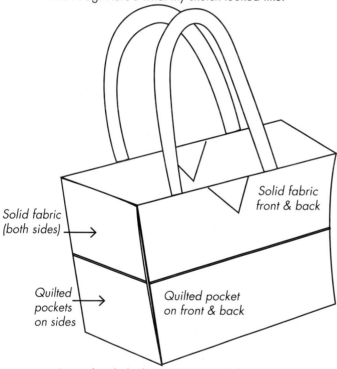

Solid fabric front & back

Solid fabric (both sides) →

Quilted pockets on sides →

Quilted pocket on front & back

First I decided what size I wanted the purse to be. The front and back pockets would need to be at least 6" deep, which meant that the solid fabric behind the pockets would have to be 2" to 3" taller. The width of the purse panels would be 12" with a "V" cut in the center. The side panels would be solid fabric with quilted pockets, and the purse would be lined with a pocket sewn to the lining. The two handles each would be 22" long.

As I began to visualize the bag and consider class time, I became aware that my design would not work. It would take too much time to crazy quilt and embellish four pieces in class and still finish the purse. So I decided to make the back a crazy quilted panel and eliminate the pocket, eliminate the pockets from the side panels and keep the front the same.

The resulting purse was similar to the original plan. However, since I feel it is important to finish a project in class, it was adjusted to fit the time in class.

THREE WAYS TO DESIGN A PURSE

To get the ultimate feeling of creativity, you will want to begin to create your own designs and patterns. It's not as hard as you might imagine. In this chapter, you will learn how to make three purses that are designed by three different methods: the Myrtle Would Handbag (Vertical Design); the Modern Myrt Handbag (Horizontal Design); and the Museum Bag I (Shaped Design).

Try these three designs to get the feel of how they are put together. Then design your own purses. It's easy and so much fun!

VERTICAL DESIGN

The Myrtle Would Handbag is an example of a vertical design; instructions for the bag begin on page 42.

The Myrtle Would Handbag is an example of a vertical design. This purse is comprised of a front panel (a quilted center with two solid pieces on each side of center); a bottom (which is a solid fabric); and a back panel (which is another solid fabric).

Side Panel	Front Panel	Side Panel
	Bottom	
	Back Panel	

You can see why this design is called vertical. The three components (front, bottom and back) of this purse line up vertically.

I wanted the finished purse to be 12½" wide by 8½" tall, with a 3" bottom. To accomplish all of this, I would have to make the front and back panels 13½" x 9½", and the bottom would have to be 13½" x 4". To make the front of the purse come out to the correct measurement, and to make it different and interesting, I first made a crazy quilted square that measured 9½" x 9½". To make the purse front the correct width, I attached a 3" x 9½" panel on each side of the quilted square. When these two panels were added using a ½" seam allowance, the result was a rectangle that measures a perfect 9½" x 13½".

When this rectangle is sewn to the bottom panel and the back purse panel is sewn to the other side of the bottom panel, the result is a rectangle that measures 13½" x 21". This also is the size of the lining, which is cut out of one piece of fabric.

Petunia is another example of a purse that uses a vertical design; instructions for the bag begin on page 64.

39

HORIZONTAL DESIGN

The Modern Myrt Handbag follows a horizontal design. You can see why this design is called horizontal; all four components of this purse line up horizontally.

This is a new version of the bag that was shown on the cover of my first book, "Crazy Quilting With Attitude." This version is comprised of crazy-quilted front and back panels and solid-fabric side panels.

I wanted the finished purse to be 11" x 8½". There is no separate bottom; the front and back panels are sewn together at the bottom. A 4" miter on each side creates a rectangular bottom.

Front Quilted Piece	Side	Back Quilted Piece	Side

To accomplish all of this, I made the front and back quilted panels 12" x 11½". Each side is 5" x 11½". When the four pieces are sewn together using a ½" seam allowance, the result is a rectangle that measures 11½" x 31". That also is the measurement of the purse lining, which is one piece of fabric.

The Modern Myrt Handbag is an example of a horizontal-design purse; instructions for the bag begin on page 46.

SHAPED DESIGN

An example using a shaped design is the Museum Bag I. A version of this purse was featured in the gallery of my first book, "Barbara Randle's Crazy Quilting With Attitude."

In this book, I am sharing the directions and pattern for this purse. The pattern is needed because there are curves, and you can't just measure pieces of fabric as you can for the purses that follow vertical and horizontal design schemes.

The easiest way to make a pattern for a shaped design is to decide the measurement you want the bag to be, draw half of the design, then place the pattern on the fold of the fabric so that both sides will be cut symmetrically.

The Museum Bag I is an example of a shaped-design purse. Instructions for the bag start on page 50, and the pattern appears on page 126.

Myrtle Would Handbag

Myrtle Would Handbag; with initial. Finished size: 12½" wide x 8½" tall; bottom is 3" wide.

Materials

Fabric

- ⅓ yd. canvas (foundation fabric)
- 7" x 7" scrap of fabric (centerpiece)
- ⅛ yd. each of 12 different fabrics (crazy quilting)
- ⅛ yd. fabric (side panels on purse front)
- ⅓ yd. fabric (purse back)
- ⅛ yd. fabric (purse bottom)
- ¾ yd. fabric (lining, grid pocket)

Embellishments and Notions

- ½ yd. ribbon or webbing, 1" wide (handle tabs)
- Magnetic snap closure
- Pair of purse handles (bamboo or other style to suit)
- Thread
- Plastic canvas or (grid bottom)
- ¼ yd. fusible interfacing
- Other crazy quilting embellishments, as desired
- ⅛ yd. interfacing

A monogrammed initial graces the centerpiece of the Myrtle Would Handbag. The purse follows the vertical design scheme, which means the front panel, bottom and back panel of the bag line up vertically.

From	Cut
Canvas	2 squares, 10½" x 10½"
Quilting fabrics	1 square, 6" x 6"
	12 strips, 3" x 10" (1 strip of each fabric)
Lining and grid	1 rectangle, 13½" x 21"
pocket fabric	1 rectangle, 4" x 9"
Purse back fabric	1 rectangle, 9½" x 13½"
Purse bottom fabric	1 rectangle, 4" x 13½"
Side panel fabric	2 rectangles, 3" x 9½"
Fusible interfacing	2 rectangles, 2" x 8½"
Interfacing	1 rectangle, 3" x 9" (purse bottom)
Ribbon or webbing	4 tabs for handles, each 1" x 3"
Plastic canvas	1 rectangle, 2⅞" x 9"

EMBROIDER

1 Embroider the initial for purse's centerpiece square onto the 7" x 7" piece of fabric.

2 Cut the embroidered piece into a diamond shape no larger than 4" on each side.

QUILT AND EMBELLISH

1 Use the Traditional technique of crazy quilting (Method 1) to add the diamond-shaped embroidered fabric to the center of the foundation fabric.

2 Use the Traditional crazy quilting technique to sew the strips of fabric to the foundation fabric. See Getting Started for detailed instructions.

3 Repeat Step 2 until all of the foundation fabric is covered with the crazy quilted fabric strips.

4 Embellish the crazy quilted fabric as desired. See Embellishments for ideas and detailed instructions.

5 Press the embellished piece well.

ASSEMBLE

EXTERIOR

1 Trim the crazy quilted piece to 9½" x 9½". Find the center of this piece; cut a notch on both the top and bottom of the piece.

2 Fuse 2" x 8½" interfacing pieces to the center of each 3" x 9½" side panel.

3 With right sides together, sew each 3" x 9½" piece of fabric to each side of the quilted piece.

4 Fuse the 3" x 9" piece of interfacing to the center of the purse bottom fabric.

5 Make center notches on both of the long sides of 4" x 13½" purse bottom. Match the center notches, and stitch the purse bottom along one 13½" side of the quilted piece (purse front).

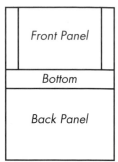

Front Panel
Bottom
Back Panel

6 Make center notches on both 13½" sides of the purse back. Matching the center notches, stitch the purse back to the opposite side of the 13½" purse bottom.

7 Press the seams open to yield a 13½" x 21" rectangle. Fold the rectangle in half, right sides together. Match the top edge of purse front to top edge of purse back.

8 Stitch both sides together from the top edge to the fold. Clip to the seam at the fold. Press the seams open.

9 Make a 3" miter at both side seams to create a rectangular bottom. Hold the side seam with one hand. Match the center of the seam to the center of the purse bottom, which will form a triangle. Pin to hold this position.

10 Measure 1½" from the point of the triangle. Draw a line across the triangle intersecting mark. Stitch across the open seam. See Bag Basics for detailed instructions. Turn the purse right side out.

11 Fold the tabs for handles in half, matching the raw ends. Baste the raw ends together to hold.

12 Measure the handles being used. Mark the front and back of the purse to indicate where to place the tabs for handles.

13 Pin tabs, raw ends up, to the right side of purse. Baste to hold.

LINING

1 Make a pocket. See Bag Basics for detailed instructions. Turn the pocket. Press.

2 Center the pocket at one end of lining fabric, 2" from top edge. Center snap parts at each end of lining, 1¼" from raw edges.

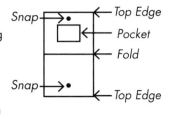

Snap → • ← Top Edge
← Pocket
← Fold
Snap → • ← Top Edge

3 Fold the lining, right sides together; match the 13½" edges.

4 Stitch both sides together from the top edge to the fold. Leave a 6" opening on one side to turn the purse through.

5 Make a 3" miter at both side seams to create a rectangular bottom. Refer to Bag Basics for detailed instructions.

6 If desired, make a pocket inside the lining across the bottom to hold the grid. See Bag Basics for detailed instructions.

PURSE AND HANDLES

1 Drop the outer purse into the lining, right sides together.

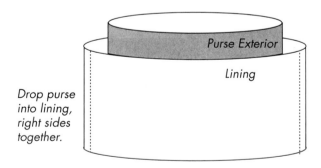

Purse Exterior

Lining

Drop purse into lining, right sides together.

2 Pin the pieces at the side seams; then pin at the centers and in between. Stitch the outer purse to the lining using a ½" seam allowance.

3 Turn the purse right side out through the opening left in the lining. Press the piece around the top.

4 Topstitch around the top of the purse.

5 Topstitch the lining opening closed.

6 Insert the manufactured handles into the tabs.

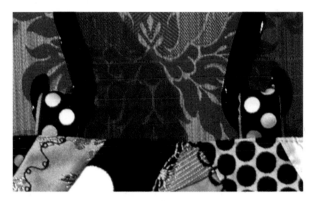

VARIATION

Myrtle Wouldn't Handbag

If you like the Myrtle Would Handbag design but would prefer different handles, try the Myrtle Wouldn't Handbag.

Make the purse and lining following the directions for the Myrtle Would purse. Use all of the same materials cut to the same sizes, except substitute one 4" x 44" piece of fabric and two ⅞" x 44" pieces of fusible fleece for the store-bought handles and ribbons/webbing handle tabs used in the Myrtle Would bag.

The finished fabric handles will be 1" x 22". See Bag Basics for detailed instructions.

To place the handles, make marks 2½" and 3½" on each side of the center notches on the purse front and purse back. Place the handles between the marks. Instead of stitching the tabs onto the outer purse, stitch the handles in place.

Modern Myrt Handbag

Modern Myrt Handbag. Finished size: 11" wide by 8½" tall; sides and bottom are 4" wide.

Materials

Fabric

- ½ yd. canvas (foundation fabric)
- ¼ yd. fabric (side panels)
- ⅛ yd. each of 16 different fabrics (crazy quilting)
- ½ yd. fabric (lining)
- ¼ yd. total fabric (grid pocket, lining pocket)
- ¼ yd. fabric (handles)

Embellishments and Notions

- ⅛ yd. interfacing (sides, snap reinforcement)
- ⅛ yd. fusible fleece, at least 36" wide (handles)
- Plastic canvas
- Magnetic snap closure
- 1 yd. fuzzy trim
- Thread
- Other crazy quilting embellishments, as desired

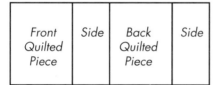

Fuzzy trim, funky fabrics and yarn embellishments lend a playful touch to the Modern Myrt Handbag. This purse follows the horizontal design, meaning the front, sides and back are joined side by side.

From	Cut
Canvas	2 rectangles, 13" x 12½"
Crazy quilting fabrics	30 strips, 3" x 10" (2 each of 15 fabrics)
	2 centerpieces, 3½" x 3½" (both from same fabric)
Side panel fabric	2 rectangles, 5" x 11½"
Fusible interfacing	2 rectangles, 4" x 10½" (for side fabrics, if needed)
Lining fabric	1 rectangle, 11½" x 31"
Pocket fabric	1 rectangle, 7½" x 13"
Plastic canvas	1 rectangle, 3¾" x 10½"
Grid pocket fabric	1 rectangle, 5" x 10½" (pocket)
Handle fabric	2 rectangles, 4" x 36"
Fusible fleece	4 strips, ⅞" x 36"

QUILT AND EMBELLISH

1 Use the Traditional technique of crazy quilting (Method 1) to sew the center fabric square to one canvas foundation rectangle.

2 Use the Traditional technique of crazy quilting (Method 1) to add the crazy quilting fabric to the foundation fabric. See Getting Started for detailed instructions.

3 Repeat Steps 1 and 2 for the second canvas foundation rectangle.

4 Embellish the crazy quilted fabric as desired. See Embellishments for ideas and detailed instructions.

5 Press each piece well.

6 Trim the quilted pieces to measure 12" wide x 11½" tall.

ASSEMBLE

POCKET AND LINING

1 Make a pocket. See Bag Basics for detailed instructions.

2 Turn the pocket. Press.

3 Stitch the pocket to the right side of the lining, positioning it 2" from the top edge of the lining and 4¾" from the right side. The purse's center is 8" from each side.

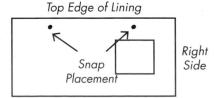

Top Edge of Lining

Snap Placement

Right Side

4 Fold the lining in half, placing right sides together and matching the side edges. Stitch the two sides together using a ½" seam allowance, but leave a 6" opening in the middle of the seam. You will have a cylinder that is open at the top and bottom.

5 Stitch across bottom, from fold to seam, using a ½" seam allowance.

6 Center and fuse 2" x 2" pieces of interfacing to the wrong side of the lining, 1½" from the top. This provides stability when securing the snaps.

7 Make a notch at the center on both the front and back of the lining. The center is at 8".

8 Make a 4" miter at both sides of the lining to create a rectangular bottom. See Bag Basics for detailed instructions.

9 If desired, make a pocket inside the lining across the bottom to hold the grid. See Bag Basics for detailed instructions.

PURSE AND HANDLES

1 Make the fabric handles. See Bag Basics for detailed instructions.

2 Place one purse side and the purse front right sides together. Sew them together along the 11½" edge. If needed, fuse interfacing to the sides.

3 Place the second purse side and the purse front right sides together. Sew them together along the 11½" edge.

Purse Side	Purse Front	Purse Side	Purse Back

4 Sew the open edge of the purse side to purse back. Press the seams open.

5 With right sides together, sew the ends of the rectangle together to form a cylinder. Press the seam open.

6 Hold the cylinder so that the front of the purse faces you, the back of the purse lines up with the front of the purse and the right sides of the fabric are together. Match the front and back side seams together on each side of purse front and back. Stitch across the bottom using a ½" seam allowance.

7 Clip to the fold at each end. Press the seam open.

8 Form a miter by matching the center of the side with the seam at the bottom of the purse. Stitch in the ditch to secure the miter.

9 Turn the purse right side out.

HANDLES AND TRIM

1 Make marks on the inside top of the quilted pieces; the marks should be 2" from each of the four side seams.

2 Make a second set of marks that is 3" from each of the four side seams. The handles will be placed between the marks.

3 With right sides together, pin decorative trim around the top edge of the purse. Stitch the trim ¼" from the edge.

4 Assemble the fabric handles. See Bag Basics for detailed instructions.

5 Pin one handle to the front and one handle to the back of the purse, placing the ends of the handles on the right side of the purse, between the marks made on the inside. Stitch the ends of handles to purse ¼" from the edge.

PURSE

1 Drop the purse into the lining, placing the right sides of the fabric together.

2 Pin the pieces together at the seams, then at the centers, then in between.

3 Stitch the outer purse to the lining; use a ½" seam allowance.

4 Turn the purse right side out through the opening in the lining. Press the top of the purse well.

5 Topstitch around the top of the purse.

6 Insert the grid in the bottom of the purse. If the grid pocket was used, insert the grid into the grid pocket.

7 Topstitch the lining opening closed.

8 Press the finished piece well.

Museum Bag I

Museum Bag I. Finished size: 10" wide x 9" tall, excluding handle and fringe.

Fabric

- ½ yd. canvas (foundation fabric)
- ½ yd. fabric (lining)
- ⅛ yd. each of 12 different fabrics (crazy quilting)

Embellishments & Notions

- 1 yd. cord (purse handle)
- ½ yd. beaded trim
- Magnetic snap
- Thread
- Other crazy quilting embellishments, as desired

The design for Museum Bag I, a shaped design, was inspired by a handbag in the First Ladies Collection at the Smithsonian Institution's Museum of American History. That bag was not crazy quilted, and it had a different handle, but the shape is what interested me. If you visit the museum, look for the purse, and as you do, notice other purses shown in the exhibit. There are some very interesting designs.

From	Cut
Canvas	2 pieces using the Museum Bag pattern on page 126; cut on the fold and allow an extra ½" around the entire pattern
Crazy quilting fabrics	2 centerpieces, 3½" x 3½" (both from the same fabric)
	22 strips, 3" x 10" (2 each from 11 fabrics)
Lining fabric	2 pieces using the Museum Bag pattern on page 126

QUILT AND EMBELLISH

1 Use a ⅛" seam allowance to sew one 3½" x 3½" square to the center of one of the canvas pieces.

2 Use the Sew and Flip method to add crazy quilting strips to the foundation fabric. Start in the center of the canvas and use a ⅛" or scant ¼" seam allowance. Press the piece well as you go. See Getting Started for detailed instructions.

3 Trim excess fabric to the size of the canvas.

4 Repeat Steps 1 through 3 for the second canvas piece.

5 Embellish the crazy quilted fabric as desired. See Embellishments for ideas and detailed instructions.

6 Steam and press the crazy quilted pieces until they are very flat. Cut each quilted piece to size, following the Museum Bag I pattern.

ASSEMBLE

EXTERIOR

1 Mark the center of the bottom of purse front and purse back.

2 Find the center of the beaded trim. Begin pinning the trim to the center of the purse bottom; continue pinning until trim is completely attached. Stitch the beaded trim to the purse.

3 Position the purse front and purse back, right sides together. Stitch the pieces together using a ½" seam allowance, leaving them open at the top. The beaded trim will be inside, between the front and back of the purse.

4 Turn the purse exterior right side out. Press the piece well; set it aside.

LINING

1 Mark the center point at the top of the purse front lining and purse back lining.

2 Fuse small pieces of interfacing ¾" below the top edge of the inside of the lining pieces, below the center mark, to add reinforcement for the snaps.

3 Add the magnetic snaps to the lining. See Bag Basics for detailed instructions.

4 Place the lining pieces right sides together. Use a ½" seam allowance to sew the pieces together along the sides and bottom; remember to leave a 5" opening at the bottom. The opening will be used to turn the purse right side out after the lining is attached.

PURSE AND HANDLE

1 Pin the raw ends of the cord up to the top of the right side of the purse at both side seams. Sew the cord ends to the purse ¼" from the top edge.

2 Drop the purse exterior, handles and all, into the purse lining. Pin the lining to the purse around top edge.

3 Use a ½" seam allowance to stitch the lining to the purse. Turn the purse right side out through the opening left in the lining.

4 Use a straight stitch to topstitch the lining opening closed.

5 Tuck the lining into the purse. Press. Topstitch around the top of the purse. Press the piece very well.

Purses and Bags,
Bags and Purses

Cover Bag

Cover Bag. Finished size: 12" wide tapering to 7½" wide at bottom x 9" tall; bottom is 2" wide.

Materials

Fabric

- ½ yd. canvas (foundation fabric)
- ⅛ yd. each of 15 different fabrics (crazy quilting)
- ⅝ yd. fabric (lining and pocket)

Embellishments and Notions

- Magnetic snap
- Plastic canvas (purse bottom)
- Purchased handles
- ½" webbing or ribbon (to hold handles)
- 1 yd. trim
- Thread
- Other crazy quilting embellishments, as desired

Cover Bag, back view.

Whether seen from the front (previous page) or back (above), the Cover Bag's fun fabrics and funky embellishments make it a showpiece. Tasseled trim and colorful striped plastic handles add a trendy twist to this shaped-design purse.

From	Cut
Canvas	2 pieces using Cover Bag pattern on page 127; add 1" to all edges
Quilting fabrics	2 squares, 4" x 4" (both from same fabric) 28 strips, 3" x 9" (2 each of 14 fabrics)
Lining and pocket fabric	2 pieces using Cover Bag pattern on page 127; add 1" to all edges 1 pocket, 7½" x 12"
Plastic canvas	1 strip, 1⅞" x 6½"
Webbing or ribbon	4 strips, 3" long

QUILT AND EMBELLISH

1 Sew one 4" x 4" square to the center of one canvas foundation piece.

2 Use the Sew and Flip method to add crazy quilting strips to the foundation fabric until the fabric is covered. Start in the center of the canvas and use a ¼" or scant ¼" seam allowance. See Getting Started for detailed instructions.

3 Trim excess fabric to the size of the canvas.

4 Repeat Steps 1 through 3 for the second canvas piece.

5 Embellish the finished crazy quilted fabric as desired. See Embellishments for ideas and detailed instructions.

6 Press and steam the embellished pieces well. Trim each piece according to the pattern outline.

ASSEMBLE

EXTERIOR

1 Place the front and back crazy quilted purse pieces right sides together. Use a ½" seam allowance to stitch them together along the sides and bottom, leaving the top open to create a pouch.

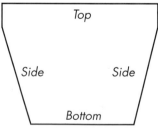

2 Make a 2" miter at both sides of the bottom of the pouch. See Bag Basics for detailed instructions.

3 Press well. Set the piece aside.

LINING

1 Make a pocket. See Bag Basics for detailed instructions.

2 Center the pocket 2" below the top edge of one lining piece.

3 Make notches at center of top of both lining pieces; the top is the widest part of the fabric.

4 Apply snaps at the center of both lining pieces 1¼" from the top edge of the lining. See Bag Basics for detailed instructions.

5 Make the lining by following the same directions as for the exterior, except leave a 5" opening on one of the side seams. The opening will be used to turn the purse through when it is put together.

PURSE AND HANDLES

1 Pin trim around the top of the outside of purse.

2 Stitch the trim ¼" from the edge.

3 Put a piece of webbing or ribbon through each end of each handle. Stitch the ends of the webbing or ribbon together to secure. Center the handle tabs onto right sides of front and back of outer purse with raw ends up. Baste.

4 Drop the outer purse, handles and all, into lining. The lining and purse will be right sides together. Pin at seams first, then the centers of the front and back.

5 Stitch around opening using ½" seam allowance, then turn the piece through the opening left in the lining.

6 Press around the opening.

7 Topstitch around the top of the purse.

8 Drop the bottom grid between the lining and the purse. Topstitch the opening in lining closed.

Elvira

Elvira. Finished size: 9" tall, excluding silk drawstring top; 6" in diameter.

Materials

Fabric

- ½ yd. canvas (foundation fabric)
- ⅛ yd. each of 10 different fabrics (crazy quilting)
- ½ yd. fabric (ruffles)
- ⅓ yd. fabric (lining)
- ¼ yd. fabric (lining bottom, pocket)
- ¼ yd. fabric (purse top)
- ¼ yd. fabric (purse bottom)
- ⅛ yd. silk (handle)
- ⅛ yd. fusible fleece (handle)

Embellishments and Notions

- ¼ yd. fusible interfacing (purse bottom)
- 1 yd. drawstring
- 2 wooden balls (for end of drawstring)
- 2 D-Rings
- ⅓ yd. ribbon, 1" wide
- Plastic canvas (purse bottom)
- Thread
- Other crazy quilting embellishments, as desired

Elvira, back view.

Ruffles, a drawstring closure and a barrel shape give a distinctive look to the Elvira bag, which is constructed following the horizontal design scheme. The crazy quilted fabric is created using Method 3, On The Slant.

From	Cut
Canvas	3 pieces, 5" x 22"
Quilting fabrics	30 strips, 3 of each color, 3" x 9"
Ruffle fabric	4 strips, 4" x 44"
Lining fabric	1 rectangle, 10" x 21"
Pocket and lining bottom fabric	1 circle, 7½" in diameter 1 rectangle, 7½" x 14"
Purse top fabric	1 rectangle, 8" x 21"
Purse bottom fabric	1 circle, 7½" in diameter
Handle fabric	1 strip, 4" x 44"
Fusible interfacing	1 circle, 6½" in diameter
Fusible fleece	2 strips, ⅞" x 44"
Drawstring	1 piece, 30" long
Plastic canvas	1 circle, 5¾" in diameter
Ribbon	2 pieces, 3½" long

QUILT AND EMBELLISH

1 Use the On the Slant technique (Method 3) to crazy quilt 10 fabric strips onto the first 4" x 22" canvas foundation piece. See Getting Started for detailed instructions.

2 Press the piece well.

3 Repeat Steps 1 and 2 for the remaining foundation pieces.

4 Embellish the crazy quilted pieces as desired. See Embellishments for ideas and detailed instructions. Press well.

5 Trim all three finished pieces to 4" x 21".

ASSEMBLE RUFFLES

1 Create four ruffles. Each ruffle should measure about 20" long after it is gathered. See Bag Basics for detailed instructions.

EXTERIOR

1 Starting ⅝" from the end of one quilted strip, pin a ruffle along the long edge. End ⅝" from the end of the strip. Stitch the ruffle ¼" from the edge to hold.

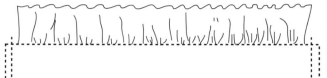

Sew a ruffle to a strip.

2 Matching the ends of strips, pin another strip right sides together on top of the ruffle stitched in Step 1. Stitch in place using a ½" seam. Press the seam open.

3 Pin another ruffle, as in Step 1, along the other edge of the strip just sewn. Stitch the ruffle ¼" from the edge to hold.

4 Matching the ends of strips, pin another strip, right sides together, on top of ruffle as in Step 2. Stitch a ½" seam. Press the seam open.

5 Pin another ruffle along both remaining raw edges of quilted pieces. You now should have a rectangle measuring 10" x 21" with a ruffle along each 21" edge and two ruffles spaced between strips.

6 With right sides together, stitch the two 10" side edges of the rectangle together using a ½" seam allowance. Press the seam open. You now have a cylinder open at both ends.

BOTTOM

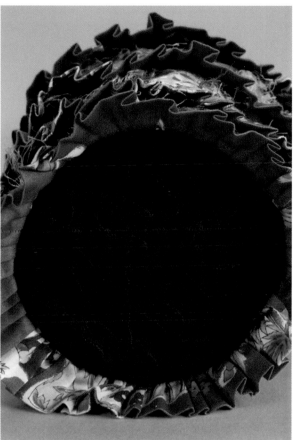

1 Fuse the interfacing cut for the purse bottom to the center of purse bottom. Make quarter-section marks on this circle.

2 Mark quarter marks on the bottom of purse cylinder. Pin the purse bottom to the purse cylinder, matching quarter marks. Clip the cylinder edge as you go to make it fit perfectly to the circle.

3 Stitch the bottom to the cylinder using ½" seam allowance. Turn the purse right side out.

HANDLE

1 Create a 1" x 44" fabric handle using the fusible fleece and handle fabric strip. See Bag Basics for detailed instructions.

Fusible Batting
Center Fold Line
Fusible Batting

2 Cut two pieces that each measure 3" long from the end of the handle strip. The handle piece now will measure 38" long.

3 Fold each 3" piece in half to make a loop. Insert one D-ring into each loop.

4 Zigzag the raw ends of each loop together.

5 Loop the purse handle through the D-rings. Stitch the raw ends to the handle, and cover the raw ends with small piece of ribbon.

6 Center the zigzagged edges of the D-ring loops at the top and bottom of cylinder over seam. Position them raw edge to raw edge.

7 Stitch the loops to the cylinder using ¼" seam.

LINING

1 Create a pocket for the lining. Refer to Bag Basics for detailed instructions.

2 Press the pocket. Pin it to the purse lining, which is 10" tall x 25" wide. Position the pocket 2¼" from the 10" edge and 2" from the 25" top edge, opening to the top edge. Stitch the pocket to the lining, leaving it open at top.

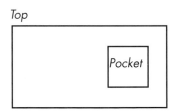

Top

Pocket

3 With right sides together, stitch both 10" side edges together; leave a 5" opening in the center to form a cylinder. Press the seam open.

4 Make quarter-section marks at the bottom of the lining.

5 Make quarter-section marks on the lining bottom. Match the section marks on the lining bottom to the section marks on bottom of the lining cylinder. Stitch the bottom to the cylinder using ½" seam allowance. Press.

Purse Top

1 Turn down ½" on the 21" edge of the 8" x 21" fabric strip. This edge will be the top. Press. Fold down another 1½" for the hem.

2 Make two ¾" buttonholes. The buttonholes should be positioned 1" from each side and 2¼" from the top raw edge.

Top

ı	ı *Hem*
	Side

3 Fold the pressed edge down over the buttonholes. Hem it with hand stitching or machine topstitching or hem stitching.

4 Stitch the sides, right sides together, using ½" seam allowance. Press the seam open.

5 Pull the drawstring cord through the hem and buttonholes.

6 Put wooden balls on each end of the cord. Knot the ends of the cord.

Purse

1 Pin the purse top to the purse, right sides together. Stitch together using ¼" seam allowance.

2 With right sides together, drop the purse exterior into the lining. The purse top (with the drawstring) should be tucked between the lining and the purse.

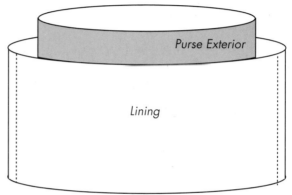

Purse Exterior

Lining

3 Pin around the top. Stitch together with a ½" seam allowance.

4 Turn the purse right side out through the opening left in the lining. Place the grid in the bottom of the purse for stability.

5 Topstitch the opening in lining closed. Press well.

Petunia

Petunia. Finished size: 5½" wide x 8½" tall; sides and bottom, 4" wide.

Materials

Fabric

- ⅓ yd. canvas (foundation fabric)
- ⅛ yd. each of 14 different fabrics (crazy quilting)
- ⅓ yd. fabric (purse back and bottom)
- ⅓ yd. total fabric (lining, pocket, grid pocket)
- ¼ yd. fabric (ruffle)
- ⅛ yd. fabric (handle)*
- ⅛ yd. fusible fleece (handle)*, at least 36" wide

Embellishments and Notions

- 1 yd. webbing*
- Magnetic snap
- ⅞ yd. woven cord, ¼" in diameter (drawstring)
- ¾ yd. ribbon (drawstring casing, drawstring slide)
- Two small tassels (drawstring ends)
- Plastic canvas (purse bottom)
- Thread
- Other crazy quilting embellishments, as desired

* You can use webbing or the handle fabric and fusible fleece to create a handle for your taste.

Petunia, back view.

Petunia came first. Then somebody wanted the same purse, just a little bit larger, so the Mama Petunia was born. The design is the same; one is just larger than the other.

Either version of this vertical design bag is quick and easy to make. The purse is quilted only on the front using the Traditional technique for crazy quilting (Method 1). Solid pieces of fabric are used for the purse back and purse bottom. I recommend using medium-weight fabrics. Use interfacing if needed.

From	Cut
Canvas	1 rectangle, 10½" x 11½"
Quilting fabrics	1 square, 3" x 3" (from 1 fabric)
	13 strips, 3" x 9" (1 each from other 13 fabrics)
Purse back and	1 rectangle, 9½" x 10½"
bottom fabric	1 rectangle, 5" x 10½"
Ruffle fabric	1 strip, 7" x 44"
Handle fabric*	1 strip, 4" x 36"
Fusible fleece*	2 strips, ⅞" x 36"
Drawstring	1 length, 30"
Ribbon	1 length, 20"
	1 length, 3"
Lining, grid pocket	1 rectangle, 10½" x 22"
and pocket fabric	1 rectangle, 7½" x 10"
	1 rectangle, 5" x 6½"
Plastic canvas	1 rectangle, 5¼" x 3¾"

QUILT AND EMBELLISH

1 Crazy quilt strips of fabric onto the foundation fabric. Use the Chevron technique (Method 2). See Getting Started for detailed instructions. Press the piece well as you go.

2 Add strips until the foundation fabric is covered.

3 Embellish as desired. See Embellishments for ideas and detailed instructions. Press well.

4 Trim the quilted piece to 9½" x 10½".

ASSEMBLE

RUFFLE

1 Fold the 7" x 44" fabric strip in half horizontally, right sides together matching raw edges. Stitch only the ends.

2 Turn the fabric right side out. Press. Overlock stitch or zigzag stitch the raw edges together. Gather the strip to create a 19" ruffle. See Bag Basics for detailed instructions.

HANDLE (OPTIONAL)

1 If desired, create a fabric handle using fusible fleece and 4" x 36" fabric strip. See Bag Basics for detailed instructions. Set aside.

EXTERIOR

1 Stitch the 5" x 10½" purse bottom piece along one 10½" side of the quilted piece.

2 Stitch the purse back along the opposite 10½" edge of the purse bottom. Press the seams open. You now have a 10½" x 22" rectangle.

3 Fold the rectangle in half, right sides together, matching the top edge of purse front to the top edge of the purse back. Stitch both sides together from the top edge to the fold, making sure seams match perfectly.

4 Make a 4" miter at both sides to create a rectangular bottom. See Bag Basics for detailed instructions.

5 Use the 20" length of ribbon or braid to make a casing for the drawstring. Start at the center front of purse. Turn under the ends, place the ribbon/braid 1" below the top edge of the purse. Leave a 1" gap between braid ends at the center front.

6 Sew the casing to the purse at the top of the braid. Lay the cord inside the casing, then stitch the bottom of the casing shut.

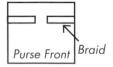

Purse Front   Braid

LINING

1 Make a pocket. See Bag Basics for detailed instructions.

2 Center the pocket at one end of lining fabric, 3½" inches from edge. Sew in place. See Bag Basics for detailed instructions.

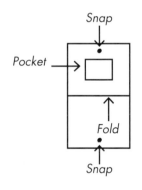

Snap

Pocket →

Fold

Snap

3 Center the snap parts at each end of lining, 1¼" from the raw edges. Install the snaps; see Bag Basics for detailed instructions.

4 Fold the lining, right sides together, matching the 10½" top edges. Stitch both sides together from top edge to fold, but leave an opening on one side to turn the purse through.

5 Make a 4" miter at both side seams to create a rectangular bottom. See Bag Basics for detailed instructions.

6 Create a grid pocket. See Bag Basics for detailed instructions.

PURSE

1 Pin the raw edge of the ruffle around the top edge of purse. Stitch the ruffle to purse, ¼" from edge.

2 Pin the handle to each side of purse, raw edge to raw edge, centered over seams. Machine baste the handle ends to purse using a ¼" inch seam allowance.

3 Drop the outer purse, handle and all, into the lining, right sides together. Pin the lining to the purse, matching sides, then centers, then in between.

4 Stitch the outer purse to lining using a ½" seam allowance.

5 Turn the purse right side out through the opening left in the lining.

6 Insert the plastic canvas grid into the grid pocket in the bottom of the purse.

7 Topstitch the lining opening shut.

8 Hand stitch tassels to the ends of the cord.

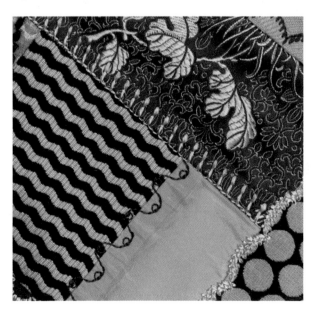

Mama Petunia

Mama Petunia. Finished size: 9" wide x 10" tall; sides and bottom are 4" wide.

Materials

Fabric

- ½ yd. canvas (foundation fabric)
- ⅛ yd. each of 16 different fabrics (crazy quilting)
- ½ yd. fabric (purse back, purse bottom)
- ½ yd. total fabric (lining, pocket, grid pocket)
- ¼ yd. fabric (ruffle)
- ¼ yd. fabric (handle)
- ⅛ yd. fusible fleece (handle)

Embellishments and Notions

- Magnetic snap
- 1 yd. woven cord (drawstring)
- 1 yd. ribbon (drawstring casing, drawstring slide)
- 2 tassels or 2 wooden balls (drawstring end)
- Plastic canvas (purse bottom)
- Interfacing (if fabric requires it)
- Thread
- Other crazy quilting embellishments, as desired

Mama Petunia, back view.

From its ruffled top to its drawstring closure, the Mama Petunia bag sports the same vertical design and features of the Petunia pattern — it's just a little bigger. While the front is crazy quilted using the Traditional technique (Method 1), both the back (shown above) and bottom of the purse are cut from single pieces of fabric, which makes construction faster and easier.

From	Cut
Canvas	1 piece 12" x 15"
Quilting fabrics	1 square, 3" x 3"
	15 strips, 3" x 9"
Purse back and	1 rectangle, 11" x 14"
bottom fabric	1 rectangle, 5" x 14"
Ruffle fabric	1 rectangle, 7" x 54"
Handle fabric	1 rectangle, 6" x 36"
Lining, pocket and	1 rectangle, 14" x 25"
grid pocket fabric	1 rectangle, 7½" x 12"
	1 rectangle, 5" x 9"
Fusible fleece	2 strips, 1⅜" x 36"
Woven cord	1 length, 36"
Braid or ribbon	1 length, 28"
	1 length, 3"
Plastic canvas	1 rectangle, 3⅝" x 8¼"

QUILT AND EMBELLISH

1 Sew the centerpiece onto the foundation fabric.

2 Crazy quilt strips of fabric onto the foundation fabric using the Chevron technique (Method 2). Add strips until the foundation fabric is covered. See Getting Started for detailed instructions.

3 Embellish the crazy quilted fabric as desired. See Embellishments for ideas and detailed instructions. Press well.

4 Trim the piece to 11" x 14".

ASSEMBLE
EXTERIOR

1 Stitch the 5" x 14" bottom along one 14" side of the quilted piece, right sides together.

2 Stitch the purse back along the opposite 14" edge of the purse bottom, right sides together. Press seams open. You now have a rectangle measuring 14" x 25".

Top Edge
Front
Bottom
Back
Top Edge

3 Fold the rectangle in half, right sides together, matching the top edge of the purse front to the top edge of the purse back. Stitch both sides together from the top edge to the fold; make sure seams match perfectly.

4 Make a 4" miter at both sides to create a rectangular bottom. See Bag Basics for detailed instructions. Turn the purse right side out.

5 Use a 28" piece of braid or ribbon to make a casing for the drawstring. Turn under the ends of the braid or ribbon. Starting at the center front of the purse, place and pin the braid or ribbon 2" below the top edge of the purse. Leave a 1" gap between the ends as they meet at center front.

6 Sew the ribbon/braid casing at the top. Lay in the drawstring cord, then stitch the bottom edge of the casing.

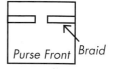

Purse Front *Braid*

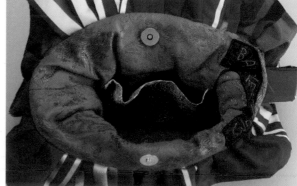

LINING

1 Make a pocket. See Bag Basics for detailed instructions. Turn the pocket, and press it.

2 Center the pocket at one end of the lining fabric, 3½" from the top edge. Sew in place.

3 Center snap parts at each end of the lining, 1½" from raw edges. See Bag Basics for detailed instructions.

4 Fold the lining, right sides together. Match the 14" top edges. Stitch both sides together from the top edge to the fold, but leave an opening on one side to turn the purse through.

5 Make a 4" miter at both side seams to create a rectangular bottom. See Bag Basics for detailed instructions.

6 Create a grid pocket. See Bag Basics for detailed instructions.

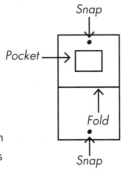

Snap

Pocket →

Fold

Snap

RUFFLE

1 Fold the 7" x 54" fabric strip in half horizontally, right sides together. Stitch the ends. Turn the piece right side out. Press.

2 Create a 26" ruffle from the sewn fabric strip. See Bag Basics for detailed instructions.

HANDLE

1 Create a fabric handle using fusible fleece and the 7" x 54" fabric strip. Fuse the fleece to the fabric, fold the fused pieces in half horizontally and press.

2 Fold the raw edges with the fleece to the fold. Press. Stitch the fabric to create a 1½" x 36" handle. See Bag Basics for detailed instructions.

PURSE

1 Pin the raw-edge of the ruffle around the top edge of the right side of the purse. Stitch the ruffle to the purse ¼" from the edge.

2 Pin the handle to each side of the purse at the seams. Machine baste the handle ends to purse using ¼" seam allowance.

3 Drop the outer purse into lining, right sides together. Pin the pieces at the sides, then at the centers, then in between. Stitch the outer purse to the lining using ½" seam allowance.

4 Turn the purse right side out through the opening left in the lining. Insert the plastic canvas into the grid pocket in the bottom of the lining. Topstitch the lining opening closed.

5 If desired, make a slide to tighten the drawstring. Sew one end of a 3" piece of ribbon around one end of the drawstring and then sew the other end of the ribbon around the other end of the drawstring. This creates a tight slide that keeps the drawstring from pulling back through the bag.

6 Hand stitch a tassel at each end of the drawstring, or thread wooden balls at the ends of the cord. If using wooden balls, tie knots at each end of the cord.

Woman's Day Book Bag

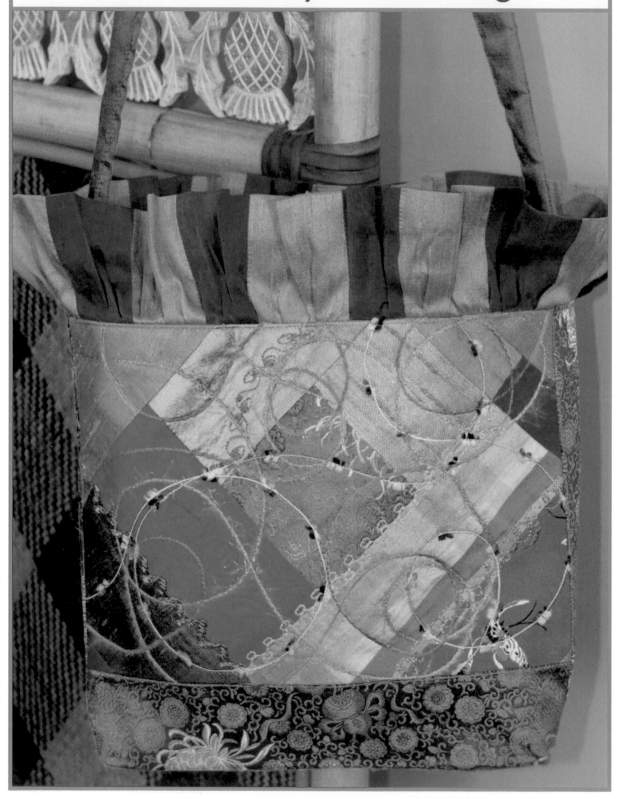

Woman's Day Book Bag. Finished size, including ruffle: 8" wide x 11½" tall; bottom is 4" wide.

Materials

Fabric

- ⅓ yd. canvas (foundation fabric)
- ⅛ yd. each of 11 different fabrics (crazy quilting)
- ⅓ yd. fabric (purse lining, pocket, grid pocket)
- ¼ yd. fabric (purse sides, bottom)
- ¼ yd. each of 2 contrasting fabrics (ruffle)
- ¼ yd. fabric (handle)
- ⅛ yd. fusible fleece, at least 36" wide (handle)

Embellishments and Notions

- Magnetic snap
- Plastic canvas (purse bottom)
- Thread
- Other crazy quilting embellishments, as desired

Woman's Day Book Bag, back view.

The Woman's Day Book Bag was designed for an August 2003 article in Woman's Day magazine. This horizontal-design purse is crazy quilted on both front and back using the Traditional technique (Method 1).

From	Cut
Canvas	2 pieces, 9" x 12"
Quilting fabric	2 squares, 3½" x 3½" (from the same fabric)
	20 strips, 3" x 10" (2 strips from each fabric)
Purse sides fabric	2 pieces, 3" x 11½"
Purse bottom fabric	2 pieces, 4½" x 11"
Lining, pocket and	1 rectangle, 11½" x 25"
grid pocket fabric	1 rectangle, 7½" x 12½"
	1 rectangle, 3¼" x 8½"
Ruffle fabrics	12 strips, 3" x 6" (first fabric)
	11 strips, 3" x 6" (second fabric)
Handle fabric	1 strip, 6" x 36"
Fusible fleece	2 strips, 1⅜" x 36"
Plastic canvas	1 rectangle, 2¾" x 8½"

QUILT AND EMBELLISH

1 Place a 3½" square on point (at a 45 degree angle) on the center of the first canvas foundation piece.

2 Crazy quilt around the square with the 3" x 10" strips of fabric until the foundation is covered. Use the Traditional technique (Method 1), following the Sew and Flip style. See Getting Started for detailed instructions about crazy quilting. Press well as you go.

3 Repeat Steps 1 and 2 for the second canvas foundation piece.

4 Embellish the crazy quilted fabric as desired. Refer to Embellishments for ideas and detailed instructions. Press well.

5 Trim the piece to 8" x 11".

ASSEMBLE

EXTERIOR

1 Stitch one purse bottom piece to one 11" side of a quilted piece.

2 Repeat Step 1 for the other quilted piece.

3 Press seams open.

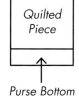

Quilted Piece

↑
Purse Bottom

4 Stitch one purse side fabric piece to the first quilted piece on the 11½" side. Stitch the other purse side piece to other side of the first quilted piece. Stitch the second quilted piece to other edge of purse side to yield a rectangle that measures 11½" x 25".

Quilted Piece	Purse Side	Quilted Piece	Purse Side
Purse Bottom		Purse Bottom	

5 Stitch the 11½" ends of the rectangle together to form a cylinder. Press the seam open.

6 Match the seams on the front and the back of purse. Pin to hold along the bottom of the purse. Use a ½" seam allowance and sew across bottom. Clip at the fold so that you can press seam open.

7 Press a crease at the center of each purse side. Miter each side at the fold. Hold the fabric at the side fold with one hand and match the center of the fold to the center of the purse bottom. This will form a triangle. Pin pieces to hold this position. Measure and mark 1½" from the point of the triangle. Make a 3" line across the triangle that intersects the 1½" mark.

8 Stitch on the line. Clip the miter triangle points off ½" from the line. Turn the piece right side out.

LINING

1 Create a pocket. See Bag Basics for detailed directions.

2 Turn and press the finished pocket.

3 Place the pocket 3½" from one 11½" edge of the lining and 2½" from the top. The lining fabric measures 11½" x 25"; the 25" edges are the top and bottom of the purse. Stitch the pocket in place.

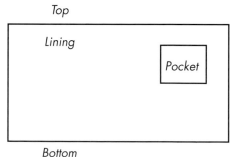

Top

Lining

Pocket

Bottom

4 With right sides together, stitch the 11½" lining edges together; leave a 7" opening in the center of the seam to turn the purse. Press the seam open.

5 Stitch the bottom edges of the lining together. Press the seam open.

6 Make a small clip at the center of the front and back of the lining.

7 Center the snaps on the lining. Place them 1¼" from the top edge; use interfacing to stabilize the fabric.

8 Miter the bottom of the lining and create a grid pocket. See Bag Basics for detailed instructions.

HANDLE

1 Create a fabric handle using fusible fleece and the 6" x 36" fabric strip. See Bag Basics for detailed directions.

2 Fold the raw edges with the fleece to the fold. Stitch the handle to create a 1½" x 36" handle.

PIECED RUFFLE

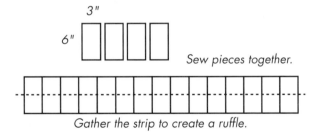

Sew pieces together.

Gather the strip to create a ruffle.

1 Use a ½" seam allowance to sew the 3" x 6" pieces together along the 6" sides, alternating colors, until the strip is 47" long.

2 Press the seams flat. Fold the strip in half, right sides together, so the piece still measures 47" long. Sew the ends. Turn the strip right side out and press.

3 Serge, overlock stitch or zigzag the raw edges together. Create a 24" ruffle. See Bag Basics for detailed instructions.

4 With right sides together, pin the ruffle to the top of the purse. Start at the center front and work around.

PURSE

1 Pin the handle to each side of the purse. Machine baste the handle using a ¼" seam allowance.

2 Drop the outer purse into the lining. Pin at the sides, then at the centers, then in between.

3 Stitch the outer purse to the lining.

4 Turn finished piece through the opening. Press.

5 Insert the plastic canvas into the grid pocket at the bottom of the lining.

6 Topstitch the lining opening closed.

Isabella

Isabella. Finished size: 13½" wide x 6" tall; bottom is 4" wide.

Materials

Fabric

- ½ yd. canvas (foundation fabric)
- ⅛ yd. each of 11 different fabrics (crazy quilting)
- ⅔ yd. fabric (purse lining, pocket)
- ¼ yd. fabric (purse sides)
- ⅛ yd. fabric (handles)
- ⅛ yd. fusible fleece (handles)

Embellishments and Notions

- ¼ yd. fusible interfacing (purse sides)
- Plastic canvas (purse bottom)
- Magnetic snap
- 1 yd. fuzzy trim
- Thread
- Other crazy quilting embellishments, as desired

Isabella, back view.

Colorful fabrics and fuzzy give a fresh feel to the Isabella handbag, which was crazy quilted using the Traditional technique (Method 1). This horizontal-design purse was created for Hancock Fabric Stores.

Crazy quilted fabric wraps around the bottom of the Isabella purse.

From	Cut
Canvas	2 rectangles, 10" x 12"
Quilting fabrics	2 squares, 4" x 4" (both of same fabric)
	20 strips, 3" x 10" (2 of each fabric)
Lining and	1 rectangle, 9" x 28"
pocket fabric	1 rectangle, 7½" x 11"
Purse side fabric	2 rectangles, 5" x 9"
Handle fabric	2 strips, 4" x 36"
Fusible fleece	4 strips, ⅞" x 36"
Fusible interfacing	2 rectangles, 5" x 7"
Plastic canvas	1 rectangle, 3⅞" x 8¾"

QUILT AND EMBELLISH

1   Sew one 4" x 4" square onto the center of one canvas foundation piece.

2   Using the Traditional technique (Method 1) add crazy quilt fabric strips to the foundation fabric until the canvas is covered. See Getting Started or detailed instructions.

3   Repeat Steps 1 and 2 for the second canvas piece.

4   Embellish the crazy quilted fabric as desired. See Embellishments for ideas and detailed instructions.

5   Steam and press the finished pieces well. Trim the quilted pieces 9" x 11".

ASSEMBLE

LINING

1   Create a pocket. See Bag Basics for detailed instructions.

2   Press the finished pocket. Find the center of the pocket by folding it in half.

3   Position the pocket so it is centered on the lining, 7¼" from the right side of the lining and 1½" from the top edge of the lining. Sew the pocket to the lining.

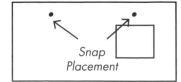

Top Edge of Lining

Snap Placement

Right Side

4   Fold the lining in half, right sides together. Match the side edges. Stitch these two sides together using a ½" seam allowance; leave a 6" opening in the middle of the seam. This should create a cylinder that is open at the top and bottom. Press the seam open.

5   Stitch across bottom from fold to seam using ½" seam allowance. Clip at the fold so that the seam can be pressed open.

6   Lay the stitched fabric flat on the ironing board. Press the side and bottom seams open.

7   Apply magnetic snaps to center front and back of lining, 1¼" from the top edge. See Bag Basics for detailed instructions.

8   Sew a 4" miter at each side to create a rectangular bottom. Since there is a seam at one side and a fold at the other, press the fold to make a crease, which you will treat like a seam when making the miter. See Bag Basics for detailed instructions.

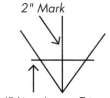

2" Mark

4" Line Across Triangle

EXTERIOR

1   With right sides together, sew one purse side to the quilted purse front, stitching along one side.

Side	Front	Side	Back

2   With right sides together, sew the other edge of the purse front to the other purse side.

3   Next, sew the other edge of the purse side to the quilted purse back.

4   Press the seams open.

5 With right sides together, sew the ends of the rectangle together to form a cylinder. Press the seam open.

6 Place the right sides of the purse front and back together. Hold the cylinder so that the front of the purse faces you and the back of the purse lines up with the front of the purse. Match the front and back side seams on each side. Use a ½" seam allowance to stitch across the bottom.

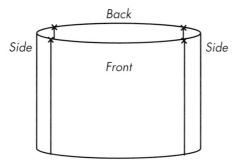

7 Clip to the fold at each end. Press the seam open.

8 Form a 4" miter. See Bag Basics for detailed instructions.

9 Turn the purse right side out.

TRIM

1 Pin the decorative trim around the top edge of the purse, placing right sides together.

2 Stitch the trim ¼" from the edge to hold it.

HANDLES

1 Create two 1" x 36" fabric handles using fusible fleece and the two 4" x 36" fabric strips. See Bag Basics for detailed instructions.

2 Mark the centers of the purse front, purse back and each side.

3 Mark the handle placements 1½" from each of the four side seams.

4 Place the outside edge of each handle on a mark. Align the raw ends of each handle with the top edge on the purse front. Pin.

5 Stitch the ends of the handles to the purse, ¼" from the edge.

PURSE

1 Drop the purse exterior — trim, handles and all — into the lining, placing right sides together.

2 Match the center marks on the lining to the center marks on the purse exterior. Pin at the seams, then at the centers, then in between.

3 Stitch the purse exterior to the lining using ½" seam allowance.

4 Turn the purse right side out through the opening in the lining.

5 Press the top of the purse well.

6 Insert the plastic canvas into the bottom of the purse.

7 Topstitch the opening in the lining closed.

8 Press the finished purse well.

Myrtle Beach Bag

Myrtle Beach Bag. Finished size: 14½" wide x 9" tall; bottom is 4" wide.

Materials

Fabric

- ⅓ yd. canvas (foundation fabric)
- ⅛ yd. each of 15 different fabrics (crazy quilting)
- ½ yd. medium to lightweight tapestry-type fabric (purse front, sides)
- ⅛ yd. fabric (purse bottom)
- ¼ yd. fabric (purse sides)
- ⅔ yd. fabric (lining, grid pocket, outer pocket, inner pocket)
- ¼ yd. fabric (handles)
- ¼ yd. fusible fleece (handles)

Embellishments and Notions

- ⅓ yd. interfacing (purse front, sides)
- Plastic canvas (purse bottom)
- Bauble or wooden balls
- 12" cord
- Magnetic snap
- Thread
- Other crazy quilting embellishments, as desired

Myrtle Beach Bag, back view.

The Myrtle Beach Bag was designed for the Smocking Arts Guild of America Sewing At the Beach Convention in Myrtle Beach, S.C., in 2004. This horizontal-design bag is crazy quilted using the Traditional technique.

From	Cut
Canvas	1 rectangle, 11" x 13"
	1 rectangle, 8" x 13"
Quilting fabrics	2 squares, 4" x 4" (both from same fabric)
	26 strips, 3" x 10" (14 for purse back, 12 for outer pocket)
Purse front and side fabric	1 rectangle, 10" x 12"
	2 rectangles, 5" x 10"
Purse bottom fabric	1 strip, 3" x 31"
Lining, grid pocket, outer pocket and inner pocket fabric	1 rectangle, 7" x 12"
	1 rectangle, 7½" x 12"
	1 rectangle, 12" x 31"
	1 rectangle, 5" x 10"
Handle fabric	2 strips, 4" x 44"
Fusible fleece	4 strips, 1⅜" x 44"
Interfacing	1 rectangle, 6" x 11"
	2 rectangles, 4" x 9"
Plastic canvas	1 rectangle, 3⅞" x 10"

QUILT AND EMBELLISH

1 Quilt one 4" x 4" square on point (at an angle) onto the center of one canvas foundation piece.

2 Use the Traditional technique of crazy quilting (Method 1) to add fabric strips to the foundation fabric. See Getting Started for detailed instructions.

3 Continue crazy quilting until the foundation fabric is covered completely. Press.

4 Repeat Steps 1 through 3 for the second canvas piece.

5 Embellish the crazy quilted fabric as desired. See Embellishments for ideas and detailed instructions. Press well.

6 Trim the front piece to 7" x 12". Trim the back piece to 10" x 12". Press well.

ASSEMBLE
FRONT POCKET

1 Pin the 12" top edge of the quilted pocket to the top edge of the outer pocket lining, right sides together. Stitch across the top edge only; use a ½" seam allowance.

2 Turn the pocket right side out. Press. The piece is finished across the top and open on the sides and bottom.

3 Machine baste the wrong sides together; sew ¼" from the raw edge around the unfinished sides and bottom to hold the lining to the quilted piece. Set aside.

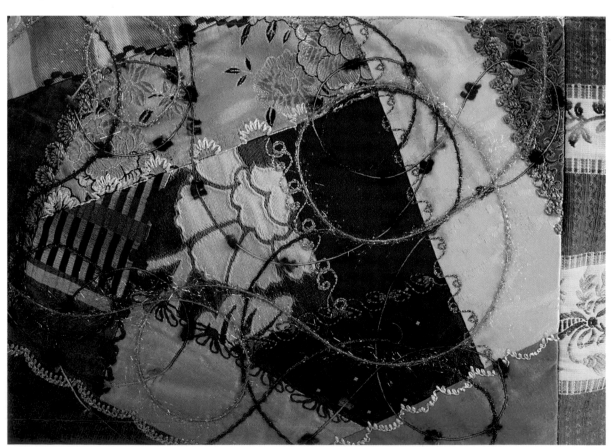

EXTERIOR

1 If interfacing is needed, stitch or fuse the interfacing to the top of the purse front.

2 Match the bottom edge of the outer pocket to the bottom edge of the solid fabric purse front, lining the side of the pocket together with the right side of the purse front. Stitch along the sides and the bottom using a ¼" seam.

Front	Side	Back	Side
Pocket			

3 With right sides together, sew one purse side to the purse front along one 10" edge.

4 With right sides together, sew the other edge of the side purse to one 10" edge of the purse back.

5 Sew the other edge of the purse back to the edge of another purse side. Press all seams open.

6 With right sides together, sew the bottom piece across the bottom of the assembled pieces. Press the seam open.

Front	Side	Back	Side
Pocket			
Purse Bottom			

7 With right sides together, sew the open ends of the rectangle together to form a cylinder. Press the seam open.

8 Align the cylinder so the front and back pieces are right sides together. Hold the cylinder so the front faces you and the back lines up with the front. Match the front and back side seams on each side of the purse front and back.

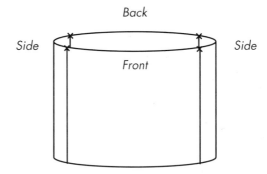

9 Stitch across the bottom; use a ½" seam allowance. Clip to the seam at each end. Press the seam open.

10 Miter each side at the fold. See Bag Basics for detailed instructions.

LINING

1 Create a pocket for the lining. See Bag Basics for detailed instructions.

2 Turn the finished pocket. Press.

3 Position the center of the pocket 8" from the lining's right edge and 2" from the lining's top edge. Stitch the pocket to the lining.

4 Fold the rectangle in half, right sides together; match the side edges. Sew the two sides together using a ½" seam allowance, but leave a 6" opening in the middle of the seam. You now will have a cylinder open at the top and bottom.

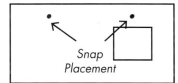

Top Edge of Lining

Snap Placement

Right Side

5 Stitch across the bottom, from fold to seam; use a ½" seam allowance.

6 Find the center by folding the fold to the seam line at the side. Make a notch at the center on the front and back of the lining.

7 Apply interfacing to the wrong side of the fabric to secure both snap components, ¾" from the top of the lining and 8" from each side edge. See Bag Basics for detailed instructions. Mark the interfacing 1¼" below the top of the lining.

8 Make a 4" miter at both sides to create a rectangular bottom. See Bag Basics for detailed instructions.

9 If desired, make a grid pocket lining across the bottom inside the lining. See Bag Basics for detailed instructions.

10 Stitch along the fabric, using a hem stitch.

HANDLES

1 Create the fabric handles using the 1⅜" x 44" fusible fleece strips and the 4" x 44" fabric strips. See Bag Basics for detailed instructions.

2 Stitch each strip to create a handle. See Bag Basics for detailed instructions.

3 Make marks on the inside top of the purse, 2¼" from each of the four sides, for the handle placements on the purse front and back.

4 Place an outside handle edge on each mark. Pin.

5 Stitch ends of handles to purse ¼" from edge to secure.

WEIGHTED CLOSURE

1 Fold the 12" length of cord in half. Thread the folded end through a loop in the bauble. Pull both ends of the cord through the fold of the cord, which will attach it to the bauble. If you are using wooden balls, thread each ball on an end of the cord.

2 If using a bauble, place the cord ends at the center of the top edge of the purse back. If using wooden balls, place the folded cord at the center of the top edge.

3 Baste the cord to the purse, close to the edge.

PURSE

1 Drop the purse into lining, placing right sides together.

2 Pin the pieces at all of the notches first; then pin in between.

3 Stitch the outer purse to the lining; use a ½" seam allowance.

4 Turn the purse right side out through the opening in the lining. Press the top of the purse well.

5 Topstitch around the top of the purse.

6 Insert the grid into the grid pocket in the bottom of the purse lining.

7 Topstitch the opening in the lining closed. Press well.

Mega/Diaper Bag

Mega/Diaper Bag. Finished size: 10" wide x 14" tall; bottom is 8" wide.

Materials

Fabric

- ⅛ yd. each of 11 different fabrics (crazy quilting)
- 2 yd. total fabric (bag lining, pocket, outer pocket lining, grid pocket, flap lining)
- ⅓ yd. muslin (foundation fabric)
- ⅓ yd. fabric (purse front, purse back)
- ⅓ yd. fabric (purse sides)
- ⅓ yd. fabric (flap)
- ¼ yd. fabric (bag bottom)
- ¼ yd. fabric (handle)
- ⅛ yd. fusible fleece (handle)

Embellishments and Notions

- 1 yd. fusible interfacing (purse front, back, sides, flap)
- ⅓ yd. nonfusible interfacing
- Plastic canvas (purse bottom)
- ½ yd. fuzzy trim (sides)
- 1 yd. beaded trim (sides, flap)
- ⅓ yd. tassel trim (flap)
- ⅓ yd. flower trim (flap; optional)
- Magnetic snap
- Thread
- Other crazy quilting embellishments, as desired

I created this bag because we were expecting another grandchild and because so many students asked for a diaper bag design. It now is a class favorite. Some people even use it as a carry-on bag when traveling. This horizontal-design bag actually is simple to make — just a lot of steps. The trick is to cut out and identify all of the pieces first. Use the Traditional technique for crazy quilting.

From	Cut
Muslin	2 rectangles, 10½" x 11½"
	2 rectangles, 9½" x 10½"
Quilting fabrics	4 squares, 4" x 4", all of the same fabric
	40 strips, 3" x 13", 4 of each color
Front and back fabric	2 rectangles, 10½" x 14½"
Side fabric	2 rectangles, 8½" x 14½"
Bag bottom fabric	1 strip, 5" x 35"
Bag lining, pocket,	2 rectangles, 9½" x 10½"
outer pocket lining,	2 rectangles, 8½" x 9½"
grid pocket and	1 rectangle, 18½" x 35"
flap lining fabric	1 rectangle, 11" x 22"
	1 rectangle, 8½" x 9½"
	1 square, 10½" x 10½"
Handle fabric	1 strip, 8" x 36"
Flap fabric	1 square, 10½" x 10½"
Fusible fleece	2 strips, 1⅞" x 36"
Fusible interfacing	2 rectangles, 8" x 10½"
	2 rectangles, 8" x 8½"
Nonfusible interfacing	1 square, 10½" x 10½"
Plastic canvas	1 rectangle, 7½" x 8½"
Fuzzy trim	2 equal lengths
Beaded trim	2 equal lengths

QUILT AND EMBELLISH

1 Crazy quilt one 4" x 4" square onto the center of the one foundation fabric piece.

2 Use the Traditional technique of crazy quilting (Method 1) to add strips to the foundation fabric. See Getting Started for detailed instructions.

3 Continue crazy quilting until the foundation fabric is covered completely. Press.

4 Repeat Steps 1 through 3 for the remaining foundation fabric pieces.

5 Embellish the crazy quilted fabric as desired. See Embellishments for ideas and detailed instructions. Press well.

6 Trim the two 10½" x 11½" pieces to 9½" x 10½". Trim the two 9½" x 10½" pieces to 8½" x 9½". Press well.

ASSEMBLE

FLAP

1 Stitch interfacing to front of the flap piece using a ¼" seam allowance around all edges.

2 With right sides together, sew front of flap to the lining along one end only. Press the seam open.

3 Lay the long flap and lining piece created in Step 2 on a flat surface. Position the piece so the lining is at one end, the flap is at the other, and the seam is in the middle.

4 Pin the tassel fringe, beaded fringe and flowers, one at a time, just above the seam on the flap front. Allow the tassels or beaded fringe to hang down over the seam.

5 Stitch each piece of trim in place, sewing from one side to the other. Depending on the trim you choose, you might put the beads on first, followed by the tassel fringe, or vice versa. Sew the flowers on top of both types of trim.

6 Fold the flap and lining, right sides together. Sew both sides with a ½" seam allowance. Leave the piece open across the top. Turn and press.

7 Machine baste across the top, ¼" from raw edges.

HANDLE

1 Using the 8" x 36" handle fabric piece and 2 pieces of fusible fleece, create a handle. See Bag Basics for detailed instructions.

2 Stitch the strip to create a 2" x 36" handle. See Bag Basics for detailed instructions.

FRONT AND BACK POCKETS (9½" x 10½")

1   Center the male side of one snap on the 10½" side of one 9½" x 10½" lining piece, 1¼" below the top raw edge. Use interfacing inside to stabilize the piece where the snap will be attached. This will be used for the back pocket. Install the snap. See Bag Basics for detailed instructions.

2   With right sides together, sew one 9½" x 10½" quilted piece to one 9½" x 10½" lining piece along the top (10½") edge.

3   Turn the pieces right side out. Press so that the pockets are finished across the top and open on the sides and bottom.

4   Machine baste close to the raw edge sides and bottoms of these pieces.

5   Repeat Steps 2 through 4 for the front pocket.

SIDE POCKETS (8½" x 9½")

1   Pin one length of beaded trim and one length of fuzzy trim, right sides together, along the top (8½") edge of one quilted side pocket piece.

2   With right sides together, pin the top of one corresponding lining piece to the top of one quilted piece.

3   With right sides together, sew the 8½" x 9½" quilted piece to the 8½" x 9½" lining piece along the top edge only.

4   Turn the sewn piece right side out. Press so the pockets are finished across the top and open on sides and bottom.

5   Machine baste close to raw-edge sides and bottom to hold.

6   Repeat Steps 1 through 5 for the second pocket.

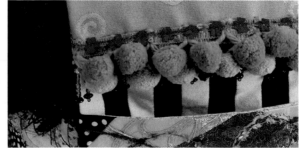

EXTERIOR

1 Fuse interfacing to the wrong sides of 10½" top edges of the front and back pieces, and the 8½" top edges of the side pieces; use a ¼" seam allowance. The interfacing only will reach 8" down from the top of each piece.

2 Stitch each outer pocket to each corresponding exterior piece, lining the side pocket to the right side of the purse, along the bottom and side edges; use a ¼" seam allowance.

3 Apply the female side of the snap to purse back to correspond with snap in pocket.

4 With right sides together, making sure pockets line up, sew one purse side to the purse front along one edge.

5 Sew the other edge of the purse side to the purse back, right sides together.

6 Sew the other edge of the purse back to the other side.

Front	Side	Back	Side
Pocket	Pocket	Pocket	Pocket

7 Press all seams open.

Front	Side	Back	Side
Pocket	Pocket	Pocket	Pocket
Purse Bottom			

8 With right sides together, sew the bottom piece across the bottom of the assembled pieces. Press the seam open.

9 With right sides together, sew the open edges of the rectangle together to form a cylinder. Press the seam open.

10 Position the cylinder so that the front and back of the purse are right sides together. Hold the cylinder so that the wrong side of purse front is facing you and the back of the purse is lined up with front of purse. Match the front and back side seams together on each side of the purse front and back.

11 Stitch across the bottom using ½" seam allowance. Clip to the seam at each end.

12 Press the seam open.

13 Miter 8" across each end. See Bag Basics for detailed instructions. Clip triangles ½" from the miter seam.

14 Turn the piece right side out. Set aside.

LINING

1 Create a pocket, refer to Bag Basics for detailed instructions.

2 Turn the pocket. Press.

3 Position the pocket 4¼" from the side edge and 2¼" from the top edge of the lining. Stitch the pocket to the lining.

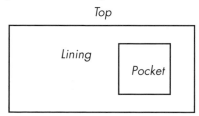

Top

Lining

Pocket

4 With right sides together, sew the side edges of the lining together; leave a 7" opening to turn. For best results, sew down from the top 3", leave the 7" opening, then sew from the bottom of the opening to the bottom of the lining. Press the seam open.

5 Stitch across the bottom. Press and clip each end.

6 Miter 8" on the bottom, as you did for the purse exterior. Trim the triangles to ½" seam. Refer to Bag Basics for detailed instructions.

7 Press creases on the inside of the lining, from miter to miter on each side.

8 Use a hem stitch to attach the grid pocket along the creases.

PURSE

1 With right sides together, pin the raw edge of the flap to the raw edge of the top of the back piece. The back piece has a snap-on pocket.

2 Pin each end of the handle to the center of the top of each purse side.

3 Baste the flap and handle ¼" from the edge.

4 Drop the purse into the lining, right sides together. Stitch the pieces together around the top; use a ½" seam allowance.

5 Turn the purse through the opening. Press.

6 Topstitch the piece around the top.

7 Put the grid piece into the grid pocket.

8 Stitch the opening closed.

Martha

Martha. Finished size: 14" tall x 8" wide; bottom is 2" wide.

Materials

Fabric

- ⅓ yd. canvas (foundation fabric)
- ⅛ yd. each of 15 different fabrics (crazy quilting, purse sides)
- ½ yd. fabric (purse pocket, lining, grid pocket)

Embellishments and Notions

- ⅛ yd. fusible interfacing (purse sides)
- Magnetic snap
- Plastic canvas (purse bottom)
- 1 yd. fuzzy trim
- 2 plastic or other purchased handles
- ½ yd. webbing (handles)
- Thread
- Other crazy quilting embellishments, as desired

Martha, back view.

In late 2003, Martha Pullen called to ask if I would teach at an event that she was planning for July 2004 in Huntsville, Ala., two hours away. We made arrangements for a purse class at the July 2004 School of Art Fashion. I wanted the purse to be an original, so I designed the — what else? — Martha. This bag also was demonstrated on Martha Pullen's television show, "Martha's Sewing Room." Use the Traditional technique (Method 1) to crazy quilt the fabric for this horizontal-design bag.

From	Cut
Canvas	2 rectangles, 11" x 14"
Quilting fabrics	2 squares, 4" x 4" (both of same fabric)
	28 strips, 3" x 10" (2 each of 14 fabrics)
	2 rectangles, 3" x 10" (from same fabric, for purse sides)
Lining, pocket and grid pocket fabric	1 rectangle, 10" x 29"
	1 rectangle, 2½" x 11½"
	1 rectangle, 8" x 13"
Fusible interfacing	2 strips, 2" x 9"
Plastic canvas	1 strip, 1¾" x 11½"
Webbing	4 strips, 3" long

QUILT AND EMBELLISH

1 Sew one 4" x 4" square onto the center of one foundation fabric piece.

2 Use the Traditional technique of crazy quilting (Method 1) to add fabric strips to the foundation fabric. See Getting Started for detailed instructions.

3 Continue crazy quilting until the foundation fabric is covered completely. Press.

4 Repeat Steps 1 through 3 for the other foundation fabric piece.

5 Embellish the crazy quilted fabric as desired. See Embellishments for ideas and detailed instructions. Press well.

6 Trim the quilted pieces to measure 13" wide x 10" tall.

7 Press well.

ASSEMBLE

LINING

1 Create a pocket. See Bag Basics for detailed instructions. Turn the finished pocket. Press.

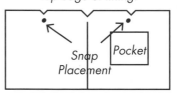

Make notches along top edge of lining.

Snap Placement · Pocket · Right Side

2 Make three notches along top edge of lining, which is 29" wide. Notches should be 7½" and 15" from the left side and 7½" from the right side.

3 Center the pocket under the notch on one end of the lining, 1¾" from the top.

4 Stitch the pocket to the lining around the sides and bottom of the pocket.

5 Fold the rectangle in half, right sides together; match the side edges.

6 Stitch the two sides together using a ½" seam allowance. Leave a 6" opening in the middle of the seam. You now have a cylinder, which is open at the top and bottom.

7 Stitch across the bottom from fold to seam, using a ½" seam allowance.

8 Fuse interfacing to the wrong side of the lining fabric to secure both snap components. Position the interfacing 7½" from each side edge and centered (the center is 7½" from each side edge and 1¼" from the top of the lining.

9 Make a 2" miter at both sides to create a rectangular bottom. See Bag Basics for detailed instructions.

10 Make a grid pocket. See Bag Basics for detailed instructions.

EXTERIOR

1 Insert snaps in place. See Bag Basics for detailed instructions.

2 With right sides together, sew one purse side to the purse front along one side; sew the other edge of the purse side to the purse back; and sew the other edge of the purse back to the other purse side. Press the seams open.

Front	Side	Back	Side

3 With right sides together, sew the ends of the rectangle together to form a cylinder. Press the seam open.

4 Hold the cylinder so the front and back of the purse are placed right sides together, and so the front of the purse faces you. Match the front and back side seams together on each side of the purse front and back. Stitch across bottom using a ½" seam allowance.

5 Clip to the fold at each end. Press the seam open.

6 Form a miter by matching the center of the side with the bottom purse seam. Refer to Bag Basics for detailed instructions. Stitch in the ditch to secure the miter.

7 Turn the purse right side out.

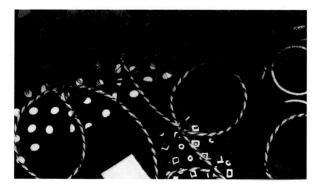

HANDLES AND TRIM

1 Find the center of each quilted piece. Make notches to mark the center point.

2 Measure the purchased handles. Mark on the inside of the quilted pieces to indicate where the handle tabs will be placed. Place the tabs appropriately.

3 Pin decorative trim around top edge of purse, right sides together. Stitch ¼" from the edge to hold.

4 Fold the handle tabs in half, matching the raw ends. Baste the raw ends together to hold.

5 Pin a tab, raw end up, on each mark. Baste to hold.

PURSE

1 Drop the purse into the lining, placing right sides together. Pin the pieces together at the seams, then at the centers, then in between.

2 Stitch the outer purse to the lining using ½" seam allowance.

3 Turn the purse right side out through the opening in the lining. Press the top of the purse well.

4 Topstitch around the top of the purse.

5 Insert the grid into the grid pocket.

6 Topstitch the opening in the lining closed. Press well.

Letter-Perfect Purse

Letter-Perfect Purse. Finished size: 12" wide x 7" tall; bottom is 4" wide.

Fabric

- ⅓ yd. canvas (foundation fabric)
- ⅛ yd. each of 7 different fabrics (crazy quilting)
- ⅓ yd. cotton or silk (lining)
- ⅓ yd. solid silk fabric (purse back)
- ¼ yd. silk fabric (monogram square)

Embellishments and Notions

- Magnetic snap
- ½ yd. webbing, ½" wide
- 2 purchased bamboo or other handles
- Plastic canvas (purse bottom)
- Thread
- Other crazy quilting embellishments, as desired

A single-fabric back cuts the sewing time for this bag.

The Letter-Perfect Purse features a classic touch — a monogram — in the center of the crazy quilted square. Use the Traditional technique (Method 1) to crazy quilt the fabric for this horizontal-design purse.

From	Cut
Canvas	1 rectangle, 11" x 28½"
Quilting fabric	14 strips, 3" x 10" (2 of each fabric)
Lining fabric	1 rectangle, 11" x 28½"
Webbing	4 pieces, 3" long
Purse back fabric	1 rectangle, 11" x 17"
Monogram fabric	1 rectangle, 6½" x 7¾"
Plastic canvas	1 rectangle, 3¾" x 8"

MONOGRAM

1   Monogram the silk fabric rectangle. Follow the manufacturer's directions for your machine.

2   Trim the monogram to a six-sided shape.

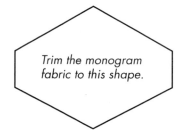

Trim the monogram fabric to this shape.

QUILT AND EMBELLISH

1   Fold the fabric in half horizontally. The fold will be one side of the purse; a seam will form the other side of the purse where the ends meet. Each end of the rectangle has a ½" seam allowance.

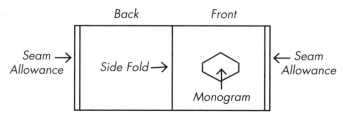

2   Measure halfway from the side fold to the seam line; this is the center front and back.

3 Center the top point of the monogrammed fabric 1" below the top edge on the front of purse. Stitch in place on all six sides.

4 Crazy quilt fabric strips onto the right side of the foundation fabric around the monogram. Lay the pieces around the monogram, sewing, flipping and pressing, until the right side is completely covered. Make sure side fold line is covered by at least ½" fabric.

5 Lay the 11" x 17" piece of silk on top of the quilted side, right sides together, at the side fold and even with the top of the foundation fabric. Stitch down the fold line. Flip and press. When placed correctly, this piece of fabric will cover the entire left side of the foundation fabric.

ASSEMBLE

EXTERIOR

1 Fold the purse, right sides together, at the side fold, matching the sides. Use a ½" seam allowance to stitch the sides together and stitch across the bottom.

2 Clip the seam allowance at side fold so that the bottom seam can be pressed open. Press the side and bottom seams open.

3 Make a 4" miter at the seam and fold sides to create a rectangular bottom. See Bag Basics for detailed instructions.

LINING

1 Make a pocket. See Bag Basics for detailed instructions.

Use Monogram Wizard Plus or another program to create monograms.

2 Turn the pocket right side out. Press. Stitch the pocket to the center of the back of the rectangular lining fabric. Leave a 6" opening on the side seam.

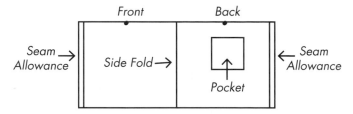

3 Construct the lining the same way you constructed the exterior.

4 Apply magnetic snaps to the front and back center of the lining, 1¼" from the top edge.

HANDLES

1 Measure the space between each side of each purchased handle.

2 Place the four tabs symmetrically on front and back of purse, with fold-side down and raw edges matched with the top edge of the right side of the purse. Sew ¼" from the edge to hold.

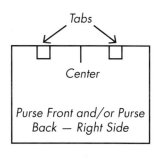

PURSE

1 Drop the purse into the lining, right sides together. Match the centers and seams.

2 Stitch around the top of the purse. Place the grid in the bottom of the purse for stability.

3 Turn the purse right side out through the space in the lining. Sew the lining space closed. Press the finished purse.

4 Insert handles into tabs.

A Gallery of Garments and Other Fun Things

Crazy Quilted Pants

Linda Sims models a colorful pair of Crazy Quilted Pants.

The inspiration received from crazy quilting can send us in many different directions. The idea to crazy quilt a pair of pants came to me a couple of years ago. Since I never have learned to fit myself with a pattern, I went to my closet and found a pair of pants that fit me well, but that I never would wear again. I made sure that the pants I used had an elastic waistband.

RECREATE THE LOOK
CRAFT A PATTERN

1 Use a seam ripper to take the pants apart stitch by stitch to create a new pattern that you will use as a guide when cutting the muslin foundation fabric pants pieces.

CUT AND QUILT

1 From muslin foundation fabric, cut two pant fronts and two pant backs that are 1" larger than the pattern.

Cut out four foundation fabric pants sections from muslin.

2 From the quilting fabrics, cut four rectangles that are as wide as the top of the pattern piece and 8" tall. Fold this rectangle in half, matching up the 8" sides. Cut the piece at an angle from the fold to the edge. When you unfold the piece, it will come to a point in the middle. Sew an altered rectangle to the top of one muslin foundation piece.

3 Starting at the top of the pants piece, quilt 3" wide strips onto the foundation fabric following the Chevron style of crazy quilting (Method 2). Some strips will be longer than others, so cut the length as you go based on the area being covered.

4 Repeat Steps 1 through 3 for the remaining pants pieces.

EMBELLISH

1 Embellish finished pants pieces as desired.

2 Press finished piece well.

SEW

1 Sew the pants together. Fold the top band over to encase the elastic, or use a drawstring. Hem the pants bottoms.

Place the first piece of fabric onto the pants piece.

Crazy quilt the strips onto the foundation fabric.

Quattro Curves Jacket

Pete Partin models a Quattro Curves Jacket she made.

A Grainline Gear pattern by Lorraine Torrence was used to create this jacket. See Resources on page 128 for more information about Lorraine Torrence/Grainline Gear.

Jazzed-Up Jacket

Morgan Freeman models the Jazzed-Up Jacket.

An old jacket that I found in my closet got a marvelous makeover. One sleeve was removed and crazy quilted. It then was stitched back together and reattached to create the Jazzed-Up Jacket.

Embellished Skirt and Blouse

Becky Jones models her crazy quilted coordinates, the Embellished Skirt and Blouse.

Becky Jones came up with the idea of embellishing a ready-made outfit with a crazy quilted design.

She also crazy quilted the tabs on the blouse of the outfit. This was done by removing the tabs, taking them apart, quilting, putting the tabs back together, then reattaching them to the blouse.

Becky took a skirt that already had a band around the bottom. With her seam ripper, she took the band off of the skirt and used it as the foundation fabric.

RECREATE THE LOOK

QUILT AND ASSEMBLE

1 Sew a four-sided piece of fabric in the center front of the foundation fabric.

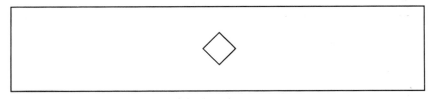

Center the square on the front of the band.

2 After adding the center piece and first four strips to the foundation fabric, use 3" strips of fabric to continue quilting using the Chevron technique of crazy quilting (Method 2). Once the entire band is quilted, stitch it back onto the bottom of the skirt and hem.

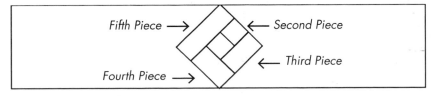

Fifth Piece →   ← *Second Piece*

← *Third Piece*

Fourth Piece →

Laptop Computer Bag Slipcover

Laptop Computer Bag Slipcover. Finished size: front, 16" wide x 12" tall; back, 16" wide x 13½" tall; flap, 16" wide x 12" tall.

Because I've been writing these books and because I've been traveling so much, my husband, Ed, thought it would be nice for me to have a laptop computer. I had no idea how handy it would be. Thanks to a wireless system, I can take the laptop on the road to work on my book. When I return home and turn my laptop computer on, it synchronizes with the desktop computer in my studio.

When I got my laptop, I received a bag to carry it in. It was a very nice black bag with extra padding inside to protect the computer. My first thought was that I needed to redesign this bag so that I would be carrying a crazy quilted laptop bag. As I examined the bag, I became aware that it would be quite challenging to make a bag that would have the reinforcement needed to protect the computer. So I began thinking "slipcover." Laptop bags vary so much from model to model; here is basic information aimed to help inspire you to create a slipcover that meets your needs.

I cut the foundation fabric pieces that were 2" larger all the way around the bag's front, back and front flap. I used 4" centerpieces and a mix of crazy quilting fabric strips — 16 on the back and 14 on the front — which I crazy quilted using the Traditional technique (Method 1). For the flap, I used eight strips, and I quilted it using the Sew and Flip method; I began in the center of the fabric and added strips as I worked my way out to the edges. My slipcover uses 3" wide gussets to fit the front, back and sides together.

Scallops add flair to the front flap. I used a peanut can as a template to create the curved edges. There also is a cutout in the top gusset fabric to allow the computer bag handle to pop through.

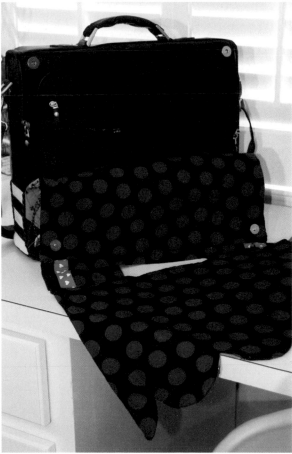

To attach the slipcover to the bag, I applied the male side of magnetic snaps to the front and back of the slipcover at each corner and applied the female component of the snaps to the actual computer bag. Another option would be to sew ties (grosgrain ribbon will do) to the top of the slipcover front and to the slipcover back, making sure the ties match up.

Travel Bags

These Travel Bags created by Linda Sims sport crazy quilted details.

Here are some travel bags Linda Sims made. She's so fancy when we take road trips!

This is a great illustration of how any pattern can be used to create crazy-quilted items. Linda created her pieces using Butterick Pattern 6263, which since has been discontinued, according to company representatives. Butterick offers other bag patterns at its Web site, http://www.mccall.com, or visit your favorite shop to find the perfect pattern for your travels.

Knitting Needle Case

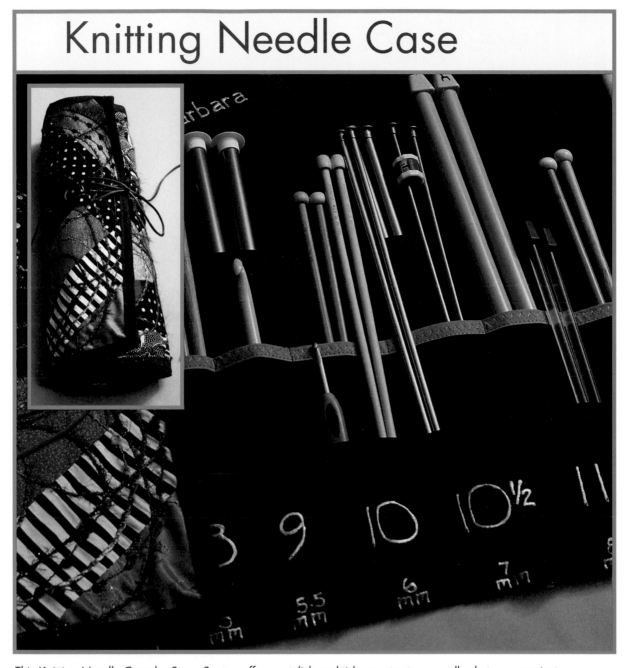

This Knitting Needle Case by Stacy Soeten offers a stylish and tidy way to store needles between projects.

On a trip to New Orleans several years ago, my Sew 'N Sew friend Celeste David visited Quarter Stitch, a wonderful knitting shop right off Jackson Square.

At the time, none of us were knitting; we just sought out knitting shops to look for yarns for embellishment of our crazy quilted projects. Celeste found many wonderful novelty yarns suitable for driving. Since then, we have stayed in touch with the nice people at Quarter Stitch. They keep us informed of new yarns,

and from time to time, they send "care packages" just to let us see what's new.

One of the ladies who used to work there, Stacy Soeten, has traveled to Birmingham, Ala., twice with her mother to take our crazy quilting classes. With inspiration received from our classes, Stacy went back to New Orleans and designed this Knitting Needle Case. The case shown in photos was given to me as a gift.

Jewelry Pouch

This Jewelry Pouch by April Jones blends a fun, crazy quilted exterior with a practical interior that offers safe and organized storage.

April Jones designed and made this jewelry pouch for her mother-in-law, Becky Jones. She crazy quilted the outside and used velvet for the lining. The pockets are clear vinyl.

Pillow and Lampshade

Becky Jones' coordinated pillow and lampshade share common colors and crazy quilted flair.

Crazy quilting is not just for purses and quilts. It also can be incorporated into lovely things for the home, like this matching pillow and lampshade. After all, creating items for home decorating is just a matter of deciding what is desired, then finding the fabric to make it happen. In this case, the fabric is a one-of-a-kind work of art created by you.

Patchwork Lampshade

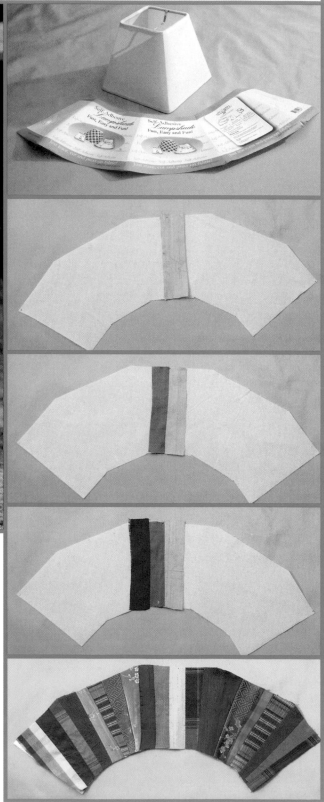

The Patchwork Lampshade adds the crowning touch to this discount-store frog lamp.

The shade that dresses up this lamp only looks hard to make. I selected several different silks that match the lamp. The self-adhesive shade's paper cover provided a pattern for the foundation fabric. I placed one silk strip, right side up, in the center of the foundation fabric piece, then attached the rest of the strips using the Sew and Flip method until the entire piece of muslin was covered. After pressing the piece well, I embellished it with reverse bobbin work, then adhered the new cover to the shade, overlapping the piece in the back. I hot-glued trim to the shade's top and bottom for a finishing touch.

Bright Idea Lampshades

Just because a lamp is a utilitarian fixture is no reason to make it bland and boring. Blend the pretty and the practical by making a crazy quilted lampshade. Whether the shade is round or square, petite or tall, once it is covered with your custom fabric and dressed up with beautiful beads, fanciful feathers or traditional trim, the lamp will add illumination and inspiration to your décor.

Beads adorn Theresa Real's Round Lampshade.

Traditional meets trendy in this Square Lampshade by Theresa Real, which incorporates beads and trim.

Feather trim gives a funky touch to Linda Burns' Round Lampshade.

Piano Bench Cover

Give yourself a comfortable and creative seat at the ivories with a crazy quilted Piano Bench Cover.

Boo Bailey had the wonderful idea to accent her piano bench with crazy quilting. This has added a beautiful look to the music room in her home. Some piano bench seats are wood, but Boo's happened to have a cushioned top. To cover a cushioned seat, try these steps.

RECREATE THE LOOK

1 Measure the dimensions of the seat. Add 6" all the way around to that measurement, and cut a foundation fabric piece to that size.

2 Begin crazy quilting in the middle of the fabric and continue quilting, following the Chevron style (Method 2) until the foundation fabric is covered. See Getting Started for detailed instructions.

3 Embellish the quilted piece as desired. See Embellishments for ideas.

4 Unscrew the seat from the frame of the bench.

5 Place the quilted piece, right side down, on a work table. Center the padded seat, right side down, on top of the quilted piece. Bring the edges of the quilt over onto the back of the seat, ensuring that the fabric is tight and even. Use a heavy-duty staple gun to staple around the edges on the underside of the seat.

6 Add trim or cording around the covered seat's edges, if desired. Reattach the seat to the bench frame.

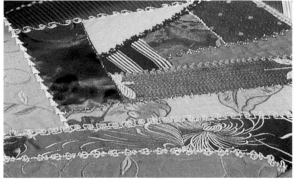

Dressing Table and Stool

Get your daily beauty regimen off to a colorful start by taking a seat at a crazy quilted Dressing Table and Stool.

A dressing table and stool that Becky Jones found at an estate sale now is a customized part of her home. A band of fabric is attached to the crazy quilted tabletop, and a gathered skirt with a front opening is attached to the band. Becky used a lightweight sheer fabric for the skirt because an air vent is behind the table, but drapery-type fabric also can be used for the skirt.

RECREATE THE LOOK

TABLETOP

1   Measure the tabletop. Use the measurements to calculate how much fabric you need. Cut the muslin foundation fabric 2" larger than the top.

2   Begin quilting in the middle of the fabric, then use the Chevron style (Method 2) to cover the entire foundation. See Getting Started for details on crazy quilting techniques.

3   Embellish the piece as desired. Press the work well.

4   Trim the crazy quilted piece so it measures 1" larger than the tabletop, which will allow a ½" seam allowance on all four sides.

SKIRT

1   Calculate the size fabric needed for a band to connect the tabletop and skirt. For the length, add up the measurements of all four sides of the table. The band's width is 5".

2   With right sides together, stitch the band to the tabletop.

3   Calculate the fabric needed for the skirt. For the length, double the total length of the band created in Step 1. For the width, measure from the band to the floor, then add 4" for the hem and ½" for the seam allowance at the top.

4   Hem the skirt fabric. Turn up ½" of fabric at the bottom, then measure from the fold and turn up an additional 3½" of fabric. Hem by machine.

5   Gather the top of the skirt. Stitch the skirt to the band so the opening is at the center front and the hem is at the floor.

STOOL

1   Unscrew the cushion from the stool frame.

2   Measure the cushion. Cut a piece of foundation fabric at least 6" larger than the cushion. Crazy quilt the piece using the Traditional technique (Method 1); begin in the middle and work out to cover the entire foundation fabric.

3   Embellish as desired. Press well.

4   Place the quilted piece right side down on a work table. Center the cushion, right side down, on top of the quilted piece. Carefully fold the edges of quilted fabric onto the back of cushion; staple the fabric to the cushion back, working to ensure that the edges are smooth.

5   Reattach the cushion to the stool frame.

Table Skirt and Square Topper

Give a side table instant drama by adding a custom cover, like this crazy quilted Table Skirt and Square Topper.

The entry hall in Linda and Dan Sims' home is made more welcoming by this exquisite round table with a floor-length Table Skirt and Square Topper.

RECREATE THE LOOK

1 Measure the diameter of the tabletop.

2 Measure the distance from the top of the table to the floor. Multiply that amount by 2.

3 Add the diameter (from Step 1) and the doubled distance amount (from Step 2). Add 2" to that total (for a hem allowance). Cut a square of fabric to that dimension.

4 Fold the square in half diagonally, then in half diagonally again to create a triangle that is four layers of fabric thick.

5 Cut a string that is one-half of the sum reached in Step 3. Place one end of the string at the point of the triangle. Swing the string across the other end of the triangle, marking the arc all the way across.

6 Cut along the line through all four layers. Hem the skirt.

7 Add 12" to the tabletop measurement from Step 1 to determine the finished size of the square topper. I recommend quilting four separate squares, and sewing them together to create the size needed. Be sure to cut the foundation fabric squares about 1" larger than they will need to be for the finished topper size.

8 Crazy quilt each square. See Getting Started for detailed instructions.

9 Embellish squares as desired, then press them well. See Embellishments for ideas.

10 Trim the squares. Sew the squares together to create one large square.

11 Cut a piece of lining fabric the same size as the crazy quilted square.

12 With right sides together, sew the quilted square to the lining, leaving an opening to turn the piece.

13 Turn the lined piece right side out. Press well. Stitch the opening closed.

14 Add trim as desired.

Crazy Quilted Seat Covers

Crazy Quilted Seat Covers add a funky touch to the seats of these two retro chairs.

Morgan Freeman has taken two fabulous retro chairs and given them new life. The lines of these chairs are so cute, and the retro fabrics used are just the right touch to take them over the top. The same procedure was used to cover these seats as was used for the stool shown on page 116.

120

Upholstered Victorian Chair

This Upholstered Victorian Chair takes crazy quilting to a new level in home décor.

When Linda Burns showed me the photo of this chair, I knew it had to be in this book. She measured how large each piece of fabric would have to be to upholster the chair, and she then "got to quilting!" After each piece was finished, she called her upholsterer to get the chair and the fabrics. So cool!

Vanity Stool and Footstool

Tasseled trim adds color to this crazy quilted Footstool.

Embellishments and crazy quilting add zing to this Vanity Stool.

These two stools were found at a local discount store for less than $20 each. They came with upholstered cushions that had wooden bottoms. To transform these ordinary items to original works of art, just cover the cushions and staple the new covers to the wooden bottom.

RECREATE THE LOOK
FOOTSTOOL

1 Measure the cushion from the edge of one side to the edge of the other side. Add 4".

2 Cut a square of muslin foundation fabric to the measurement reached In Step 1.

3 Crazy quilt the muslin, starting in the center and working your way out.

4 Embellish the piece as desired. Cover the cushion with the quilted piece, following the technique used for the piano bench and the retro chairs.

VANITY STOOL

1 Measure the piece lengthwise; add 4". Divide that measurement by 3.

2 Cut three pieces of fabric. For this project, the two end pieces are a black and cream stripe, and the center piece is crazy quilted. Cut the striped pieces larger than the desired size to allow enough fabric to create seam allowances and to secure the fabric to the bench. Cut the foundation fabric at least 2" larger than the required measurement.

3 Crazy quilt the muslin. Embellish as desired.

4 Trim the quilted piece to the desired size.

5 Stitch the striped pieces to each side of the quilted piece and staple the cover onto the cushion.

6 Use a glue gun to add trim as desired.

123

Crazy Quilted Pet Bed

This Crazy Quilted Pet Bed offers a comfortable spot for Susie to snooze.

If you have a pet dog or cat, why have a ho-hum pet bed? Why not have a pet bed that is a work of art and a conversation piece? That's just what Becky Jones did for her dogs. She found this bed at an estate sale and painted it a great color. The crazy quilted cushion is the crowning touch.

Market Umbrella

This crazy quilted Market Umbrella offers shady spot sure to dress up any deck or patio.

The original umbrella, which had a red cover and included the frame, was purchased at an import store. The cover was taken apart stitch by stitch, and the crazy quilting was done right on top of the actual pieces from the umbrella. It then was stitched back together and hemmed to create the Market Umbrella.

125

TOP

FOLD

MUSEUM BAG I PATTERN
USE ½" SEAM ALLOWANCE

BOTTOM

TOP

FOLD

COVER BAG PATTERN
ADD 1" ALL THE WAY AROUND PATTERN FOR FOUNDATION FABRIC

BOTTOM

Resources

B. Randle Designs, LLC
Phone: (205) 823-4663
E-mail: b.randledesigns@mail.com
http://www.randledesigns.com

Fabric
Decorator's Choice Fabrics
Silks, trims, beaded tassels, home decor fabrics, trims, furniture, rugs, accessories and more
612 Montgomery Highway
Vestavia Hills, AL 35216
Phone: (205) 823-1493
http://www.welovefabrics.com

Hancock Fabrics
Silks, novelty fabrics, all fabrics, trims, purse handles, general purse supplies, notions, yarns, books, furniture, accessories and more
http://www.hancockfabrics.com

Butterfly Fabrics
Silks
260 W. 39th St.
New York, NY 10018
Phone: (212) 302-2440
http://www.ButterflyFabrics.com

Hamed Fabrics
Silks
251 W. 39th St.
New York, NY 10018
Phone: (212) 302-2440

Carol Harris Co.
Heirloom, quilting, lace, buttons, trims, books and more
1265 S. Main St.
Dyersburg, TN 38024
E-mail: info@carolharrisco.com

Jackman's Fabrics
1234 N. Lindbergh
St. Louis, MO 63132
Phone: (800) 758-3742
E-mail: jackmansfabrics@accessus.net
http://www.jackmansfabrics.com

Miscellaneous
Mackenzie Childs
14 West 57th St.
New York, NY 10019
http://www.mackenzie-childs.com

Stacy Jean Designs
Needle Case for knitting needles
Stacy Soeten
Phone: (360) 943-4837
E-mail: Purpletrident@comcast.net
http://www.stacyjean.net

Fred's Pharmacy
Footstools, lamps
http://www.fredsinc.com

T.J.Maxx
Lamps
http://www.tjmaxx.com

Organized Living Store
Cubbyholes for fabric in studio
http://www. organizedliving.com

Big Lots
Vanity stool
http://www.biglots.com

World Market
Market umbrella
http://www.costplus.com

Wisconsin Lighting
Lampshades
800 Wisconsin St. Box 4
Eau Claire, WI 54703
http://www.wilighting.com

Notions
Nancy's Notions
333 Beichl Ave.
P.O. Box 683
Beaver Dam, WI 53916
Phone: (800) 725-0361
E-mail: store@nancysnotions.com

Ruthie's Notions
J.R. Barnhill Road
Baker, Florida 32531
Phone: (888) 448-4548
http://www.ruthiesnotions.com

Patterns
The Sewing Workshop
Linda Lee
E-mail: dezynn@aol.com
http://www. sewingworkshop.com

Ghee's
Linda McGehee
Handbag patterns, hardware, sewing notions
http://www.ghees.com

Lorraine Torrence Designs
Grainline Gear
2112 S. Spokane St.
Seattle, WA 98144
Phone: (800) 369-4974
Fax: (206) 725-6362
http://www.lorrainetorrence.com
http://www.grainline-gear.com

McCall Pattern Co.
Vogue Patterns
Butterick Patterns
McCall Patterns
http://www.mccallpattern.com

Photography
Sylvia Martin
Phone: (205) 592-7119
E-mail: sylvia7119@aol.com

Publications
KP Books
700 E. State St.
Iola, WI 54990-0001
Phone: (800) 258-0929
E-mail:
BooksCustomerService@fwpubs.com

Southern Lady Magazine
1900 International Park Drive
Suite 50
Birmingham, AL 35243
Phone: (205) 995-8860
http://www. southernladymagazine.com

Threads Magazine
63 S. Main St.
P.O. Box 5506
Newtown, CT 06470
Phone: (203) 426-8171

Woman's Day Magazine
http://www.womansday.com

Sewing Machine Companies
Bernina of America
http://www.bernina.com

Elna
http://www.elna.com

Janome
http://www.janome.com

Pfaff
http://www.pfaffusa.com

Baby Lock
http://www.babylock.com

Viking
http://www.husqvarnaviking.com

Trimmings
Daytona Trim
251 West 39th St.
New York, NY 10018
Phone: (212) 354-1713

M & J Trim
1008 Sixth Ave.
New York, NY 10018
Phone: (212) 391-6200
E-mail: info@mjtrim.com
http://www.mjtrim.com

Yarns
Memory Hagler Knitting, Etc.
712 Chestnut St.
Vestavia Hills, AL 35216
Phone: (205) 822-7875
E-mail: memory@memoryhagler.com

Serendipity Needleworks
2113-B University Blvd.
Tuscaloosa, AL 35401
Phone: (205) 758-0108
E-mail: serendipityshop@bellsouth.net
http://www. serendipityneedleworks.com

Knit Nouveau
4094A Helena Road
Helena, AL 35080
Phone: (205) 664-5858
http://www.knitnouveau.com

Quarter Stitch
630 Chartres St.
New Orleans, LA 70130
Phone: (504) 522-4451
E-mail: quarterstitch@quarterstitch.com
http://www.quarterstitch.com